The Journey to Find

My Divine Design

THE JOURNEY TO FIND
MY DIVINE DESIGN

ELIZABETH MAY BENNETT

WordCrafts Press

The Journey to Find My Divine Design
Copyright © 2025
Elizabeth May Bennett

ISBN: 978-1-967649-28-0

Published by WordCrafts Press
Cody, Wyoming 82414
www.wordcrafts.net

For every Christian who has lost sight of their why.

To my parents, Bob and Patty,
thank you for leading me to Jesus.

And to my husband, Daniel,
your steady, unconditional love reflects God's heart for me.

Contents

What Is Divine Design?

*D*o you know that God has prepared a divine design for your life that includes your purpose for being here and how to live it out? Better question: do you know how to find that life?

In order to discover our divine design, we first have to find Jesus Christ. Just open the door of your heart and let Him into your world.

That's the first step. But once you've done that, there's so much more.

Jesus Christ feeds, clothes, waters, fills, heals, protects, guides, restores, and overflows you. He makes you shine. He brings you light. That is your divine design.

Let me share with you how I found acceptance, worth, forgiveness, and satisfaction in who I am. As you read, ask the Holy Spirit to help you along your path to discovering your own divine design.

In the following pages you will find suggestions. This book is not a to-do list of things you *have* to accomplish. But these suggestions have worked for me. When I do them, I have more peace, comfort, and joy in Jesus Christ.

I don't follow all these suggestions every day of my life. But I try to. And I believe that's enough. I belong to Jesus Christ, and He won't lose me. When we trust in Christ, He works in us, encouraging us to come along with Him. And when we follow, we enter the exciting world of our very own divine designs.

Chapter 1

PRAY

Dear God, it's me. I'm not sure what to say. I'm not even sure who you are right now. But here I am. Show me what You want me to see.

I am a teacher. I can break down steps to do most anything to the very basic level and teach students in a way that even the most novice student can learn how to do things well. I hope to teach you about prayer in the same way.

I don't know where you are in your prayer life or how well you know the steps. But let me make it simple by explaining the basics.

In *Winning the War of Your Mind,* author Craig Groeschel talks about how each of his children approaches him differently. He loves them all the same, but they communicate to him in different ways. Similarly, our heavenly Father wants us to communicate with Him in our own unique way.

The moment you accept Jesus as your Savior, you become God's beloved child. Therefore, you can approach him like a child, any time of the day or night, in whatever way works for you.

When I was a child, after my mother tucked me into bed, she prayed with me. Since I sometimes had bad nightmares, I often prayed, "Dear God, thank You for today and please don't let me dream." I continued saying that prayer through my preadolescent years.

When I was twelve, the youth pastor at our Baptist church in Fort Worth, Texas, gave me a book that taught a specific order of prayer. It said that we should start by praising God for His sovereignty. Then thank Him for the things we have. Next ask for forgiveness of any sins we're aware of. After that we should pray for others. Last came prayers for ourselves.

I can see how this could be a good place to start, especially for people who like lists. But now that I understand God better, I realize that the order isn't important. We can approach Him using our own communication style, whatever that might be.

During my teen years I didn't pray much. God was pretty much on a back burner for me, and I only pulled Him to the front when I wanted something. *Lord, let me pass this test. Help me feel better. Make my boyfriend call me.*

By the time I hit my twenties, I'd been married and divorced. Life wasn't working out like I wanted. I still believed in Jesus and attended church occasionally. And I still prayed to God … when I needed or wanted something.

Somewhere in my thirties I realized that I didn't really have a relationship with God. I accepted what my parents and other people had told me about God without getting to know Him for myself. It was time for me to have my own testimony.

Knowing I had to begin with prayer and Scripture, I got a piece of paper and wrote down the questions I had about God. After praying about them, I was led to certain Scripture in the Bible.

The process unfolded like any other relationship in life. When we meet someone for the first time, we usually ask questions like "What is your name? What do you do for a living? Do you have a family?" The difference is that God communicates to us in a limitless variety of ways. Sometimes His voice is audible. However, for me, more often He speaks through Scripture, other people, sermons, books, or music.

I based my prayer life on these verses and still do:

> *Be anxious for nothing, but in everything by prayer and supplication, with thanksgiving, let your requests be made known to God; and the peace of God, which surpasses all understanding, will guard your hearts and minds through Christ Jesus.*
>
> ~Philippians 4:6–7 NKJV

*And whatever you ask in My name, that I will do, that
the Father may be glorified in the Son.*

~John 14:13 NKJV

*If you then, being evil, know how to give good gifts to your
children, how much more will your Father who is in heaven
give good things to those who ask Him!*

~Matthew 7:11 NKJV

After some time, I bought a prayer journal. I wrote down
all my worries and prayer requests in it. That way I could go back
from time to time and look at all the prayers God had answered.

Eventually, I started writing out my prayers like letters. I'd
open with "Dearest heavenly Father," then record the date. My
prayers soon became more personal. I realized that God knows
me completely, so why hold anything back.

I love going back and reading about my struggles, my prayers,
and my thoughts and seeing how God responded to them. Sometimes He answered the way I thought He would, other times He
answered in unexpected ways. But I knew without a doubt that
He was listening to me.

I can share the following story with you because I prayed and
journaled throughout the process.

In 2011, my husband and I lived in a mobile home park.
We owned twenty-five acres of land in a nearby town and hoped
to build a house there one day, but financial constraints and the
building market had prevented that.

One afternoon, some friends suggested we look at a house
across the road from our property that had been foreclosed about
three years earlier. The brick house sat on a hill and had an amazing
view. It was exactly what we wanted.

We made some phone calls but could not determine who held
the deed. We discovered that several people had tried to find out
with the same lack of results. So I started journaling and praying
about it.

When I told my mother what I was doing, she asked if I had

"Jericho'd" it. When I asked what she meant, she replied, "I think you should walk around that house and pray seven times, like God's people did with Jericho." The idea seemed crazy, but why not?

We asked some friends to join us. We prayed and marched around the home.

Over the next year, my husband and I had a couple of opportunities to purchase other homes. Each time, I got out my journal and prayed, "God, if this is what You want, let it work out. But if that house on the hill is meant to be ours, let this deal go." Neither deal went through.

When we got word that the house we wanted was finally on the market, we prayed about how much to offer and then placed a bid. Over the next ten days, I prayed consistently. On the tenth day we found out that no bids had been accepted. We raised our bid and prayed more. Within twenty-four hours they counter-offered, and we accepted! The house on the hill was ours.

I wouldn't be able to tell you all the details of this story if I hadn't written about it in my prayer journal.

We can ask our loving Father in heaven for *anything* in Jesus's name! And He will give us peace and good gifts. We don't always know what *kind* of good gifts we'll get. But if we ask for something and don't receive it, He has His reasons for withholding it.

When I was a kid and I asked my parents for something I knew they could give me, but they didn't, it bothered me. It distresses me even more if I ask God for something and He doesn't give it. After all, isn't He the author and sustainer of all things? Doesn't he own everything? If He loves me, why would He not want to give me whatever I want?

Let's look at the story of Job.

Job was blameless—a man of complete integrity. He had seven sons and three daughters. He owned seven thousand sheep, three thousand camels, five hundred teams of oxen, and five hundred female donkeys. He also had many servants. He was the richest person in the entire land of Uz.

One day the members of the heavenly court presented themselves before the Lord, and Satan, the Accuser, came with them.

"Where have you come from?" the Lord asked Satan.

Satan answered, "I have been patrolling the earth, watching everything that's going on."

The Lord asked, "Have you noticed My servant, Job? He is the finest man in all the earth. He fears Me and stays away from evil."

Satan replied, "Well, Job has good reason to fear You. You've put a wall of protection around him, his home, and his property. You've made him prosper in everything he does. Look how rich he is! But if You take away everything he has, he will surely curse You to Your face!"

The Lord agreed that Satan could test Job. "Do whatever you want with everything he possesses, but don't harm him physically."

As the story continues, we see that God allowed Satan to test Job twice. I've got to admit, that scares the life out of me!

In the end, God gave Job back what he lost many times over. But I can't help but tremble in fear that God might allow me to be tested like that. I know people who have suffered the death of a child. I can't even begin to imagine losing multiple children as well as everything I own—all in one day.

In 2019, I went back to college to work on a master's degree. I wrote a thesis on the role of prayer for parents before and after the death of a child. I learned that prayer was the parents' best channel to grow in their relationship with God, which helped them make sense of their situation and enabled them to find peace, even to thank God for the time they'd had with their child. In some cases, God answered their prayers for peace through visions, dreams, and nature.

Some parents who experience the death of a child decide not to engage in prayer. They turn away from God, blaming Him for this unspeakable horror. But the God who made everything in nature, and who can create hurricane winds that uproot a gigantic tree in an instant, is exactly where we should turn in our grief. Because, as the story of Job shows, God is the ultimate source of comfort, peace, and blessings beyond measure.

We can find many excuses not to pray or to blame God. But that hurts us more than it does Him. When bad things happen, I do sometimes get angry at God, but I still pray. It is my lifeline to a greater power and wisdom that grants more love, joy, and peace than I could ever experience on my own.

Prayer is simply talking to God about whatever is on your mind and heart, then listening for His response. This is one of the most precious gifts available to every child of God because of Jesus Christ.

If you're not sure you believe in Jesus, ask God to grant you the gift of faith in Him. You could pray something like this:

> *God, I know I am a sinner, and I can't change myself. I have doubts and uncertainties. Your Word says that You sent Your Son to earth to live in a human body and die to pay the penalty for my sins. I want to understand what this means. Please help me in this journey. In Jesus's name, amen.*

If you are just starting out on your prayer journey, then you might want to find someone that could pray with you or be a prayer warrior for you.

My mother is an amazing prayer warrior. She prays Psalms over me and my family all the time.

My mom taught elementary school for twenty-five years, and she was so well known for her answered prayers, the administration consistently asked her to anoint the desks with oil before any major testing. She didn't do it because she believed there was power in the oil. But anointing was an act of faith that God would show up for those students and the school.

My mom will stop and pray just about anywhere—at work, in the mall, or sitting at a rest stop waiting for her husband to come out of the bathroom. It's her spiritual gift, and she knows how to use it.

The year my mother retired from teaching, I started teaching at a different school in our small community. Her assistant principal was my assistant principal. One day, she asked if my mom could come and pray because a big test was coming up. Of course, she agreed.

As she and my dad anointed the desks with oil and prayed, I watched closely to see how she did it. I knew the torch was being passed and that I would someday do this for my school. Sure enough, a year later, the assistant principal asked me to anoint the desks with oil before a major test. I hesitated at first. But my mom told me I have the same power she does.

That may be true. But when I feel the need for powerful prayer, I call her! She has a track record for answered prayers.

Recently, Mom prayed with someone to get an interview for a job he wanted. Within two days, he did. She then prayed that person would have an answer about the job by the end of the day. He did.

I hope you have a powerful prayer warrior in your life too.

Of course, my mom's prayers don't always result in favorable outcomes, but she has the spiritual discernment to know what prayers are needed at any time.

Based on my past experiences, I have come to realize that I cannot live out my divine design without prayer. I am thankful that I had parents who encouraged me to learn more about God, pray, and understand the various ways He communicates His love for me.

I encourage you to find time to pray to God. Just open your heart to Him and then look for the different ways that He will communicate to you that He hears, answers, and loves you.

Chapter 2

Control Your Mind

*I*f you want to pursue your divine design, start by considering what you believe about yourself.

On good days, I view myself as God's daughter. I know that I am forgiven, accepted, and worthy because of Christ. I believe that I am talented, smart, and wise. I am beautiful and strong. I'm a good writer, a good mom, a good grandma. I'm a good person who wants to love others.

On a bad day I see myself as lazy, tired, incapable. I am fat and unhealthy. I'm a bad mom and grandma. I am a hopeless sinner.

Now, which perspective do you think will help me accomplish what God has in mind for me? The answer is obvious. So why do I, and so many others, struggle with thinking good things about ourselves? Maybe because we don't take the time to analyze our thought process.

For the most part, we let the world tell us how to feel about ourselves. We watch TV shows and movies, commercials, and ads, and allow their subtle messages to seep into our minds.

We also let comments from other people affect our thoughts.

When I first moved to Florida from Texas, I was thirteen years old. I remember standing in the back of our moving truck when a boy was walking down the sidewalk. He started up a conversation with me. He asked where I was from. I told him Texas. His next comment has stuck with me for the past forty or so years, "I heard big things come from Texas."

I was already feeling insecure about my weight, not that I was even overweight at the time. His comment resonated within me and made me feel big. I have taken that comment with me and allowed it to shape the way I feel about my body.

Our own self-talk can either affirm or deny all the external messages we receive.

Analyze Your Thoughts

Take some time right now to analyze your thoughts. Put this book down, grab a notebook or journal, and write down what thoughts have come into your head since you got out of bed this morning. Where do you think they came from?

When we or others say something negative about us, we can focus on it until we feel terrible about ourselves. Or we can analyze those comments and our reactions and determine whether thoughts are bringing life or death to us.

Negative thoughts about yourself grieve the spirit. Thoughts that bring you peace, joy, happiness, health, laughter, love, self-discipline, contentment, and empathy toward others bring life and are pleasing to the Lord. Such thoughts can bring life not just to yourself but to those around you as well.

Where Do Thoughts Come From?

Before we can capture *death* thoughts and reprogram them into *life* thoughts, we need to understand where those thoughts are coming from.

For many years I struggled with self-esteem issues. I could always find something about myself that needed fixing, whether it was my body, my home, my walk with God, my relationships with others, my finances—the list was never-ending.

As I transitioned from childhood to adolescence, I became very self-conscious about my weight and other aspects of my appearance. I also started feeling like I didn't quite measure up in many areas of my life.

When my family lived in Mesquite, Texas, I tried out for the drill team. Thirteen girls were vying for twelve spots. I learned a dance to the song "Celebration" by Kool and the Gang, practicing it over and over in the front room. I was the one person who didn't make the team. I wasn't good enough.

Since then, there have been several situations that reinforced that belief. The feeling of never being good enough hovered over me like a dark cloud for many years.

Because I struggled with insecurity, I often wondered why God would love me or accept me with all my imperfections. These negative thoughts sent me into depression.

Perhaps you don't believe there's any way you can control your thoughts. But let me give you an example.

I love my husband and would never consider going after someone else. Occasionally I'll see a man who looks cute to me. But I never go further with that line of thinking. I don't spend another moment thinking about him.

If I know better than to entertain thought about men who aren't my husband, why can't I stop other thoughts that go against God's Word? Scripture says we are to think on things that are true, honorable, right, pure, lovely, and admirable, things that are excellent and worthy of praise (Philippians 4:8–9).

Fight Back!

If you find yourself dealing with negativity regarding a certain situation, look for Bible verses to combat those thoughts. Tell Satan to get behind you, quote the verse, and move forward.

When the devil tries to tell me I'm not good enough, I turn to the book of Ephesians and write statements about myself based on what I read there. Here are a few examples:

- I am holy.
- I am without fault in God's eyes.
- I am God's child.
- I have the same mighty power within me that raised Christ from the dead.
- God loves me.
- God chose me before I was born.
- I am God's masterpiece.

- I am a brand-new creation because of Christ.
- I am united with God through Christ.
- I am a member of God's family.
- I am God's house.
- I am bold.
- I am confident.
- I have God-given gifts.
- I have a new nature.
- My nature is righteous and holy.
- The light of Christ lives inside me.
- I am filled with the Holy Spirit.

Here are some other statements about myself, based on Scriptures, that I've written in a notebook I titled "Who am I?"

- I am clothed with strength and dignity and laugh without fear of the future. (Proverbs 31:25)
- I am always filled with the fruit of my salvation: the righteous character produced in my life by Jesus Christ. (Philippians 1:11)
- I am selfless, I am humble, and I think of others as better than myself. (Philippians 2:3)
- I am holy. I belong to Christ. (Philippians 1:1)
- God is working in me, giving me the desire and power to do what pleases Him. (Philippians 2:13)
- I am a defender of the good news. (Philippians 1:16)
- I have a confident hope in Christ. (Ephesians 1:18)
- I am a citizen of heaven, where the Lord Jesus Christ lives. (Philippians 3:20)
- I am complete through my union with Christ. (Colossians 2:10)
- I am alive with Christ. (Colossians 2:13)
- I have peace with God. I am in His presence and am holy and blameless as I stand before Him without a single fault. (Colossians 1:20, 22)
- Christ lives in me. (Colossians 1:27)
- I am clothed with love. (Colossians 3:14)

12

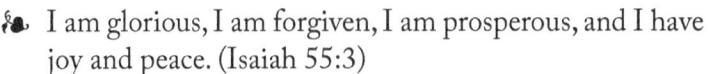
- I am glorious, I am forgiven, I am prosperous, and I have joy and peace. (Isaiah 55:3)
- I am wonderfully complex and marvelous. (Psalm 139:14)
- I am precious in God's sight. (Psalm 139:17)
- I have a spirit of power, love, and self-discipline. (2 Timothy 1:7)

Reading those words gives me a major spiritual pump-up, like what happens physically when I go to the gym. After working on my biceps and triceps for several sets, I feel confident and energetic, like my muscles are bulging. When I work on my spiritual muscles, I get a spiritual confidence boost.

If you want to build your physical strength, you need to work out at least twice a week. But we can get a spiritual pump-up seven days a week!

Here are a few ways to accomplish this that are working for me:

- I write Scripture verses on postcards and place them where I will see them throughout the day.
- I take notebooks filled with inspirational writings wherever I go and read them when I'm waiting for appointments.
- When I exercise or clean the house, I listen to Christian music.
- Whenever I come across a Scripture passage that talks about who I am as a follower of Christ, I add it to my little notebook. If I start mentally condemning myself, I pull out that notebook and read those verses. I've done that so often now, I can recall some of them by memory.

What ways can you think of to incorporate positive meditation into your life? Here are a few ideas:

- Find some favorite Scriptures, record yourself saying them on your phone, then listen to them on your way to work.
- Write a special verse on a card and carry it with you all day, reading it and pondering it whenever you can.
- Memorize a verse so you can recall it anytime, anywhere.

- Write verses on Post-It notes and tape them to your mirror, fridge, car dashboard, desktop, wherever you look most throughout the day.
- Keep a notebook full of your favorite verses and read them multiple times throughout the day. Set an alarm for certain times of the day (for example, breakfast, lunch, and dinner) to remind you to get out your notebook.
- Put tabs in your Bible on passages that bring you joy, comfort, and peace. Keep that Bible nearby all day so you can read those passages over and over.
- Ask God to help you come up with other ideas for ways you can incorporate meditative practices into your life. Try different approaches and see what works best for you.

Walk After the Spirit

The Bible is the living Word of God. It breathes life into those who seek its truths.

Romans Chapter 8 is one of my favorite Scripture passages. But it can be confusing if taken out of context.

For example, the first verse, in the New Living Translation, says, "There is now no condemnation for those who belong to Christ Jesus." The King James Version translates that verse this way: "There is therefore now no condemnation to them which are in Christ Jesus, who walk not after the flesh, but after the spirit." So, the NLT says there is no condemnation for those who "belong to Christ Jesus." But the KJV says that's true for those who "walk after the spirit." Walking after the spirit is the opposite of walking toward the flesh.

I have been saved since I was eight years old. I've had the Spirit of God living inside me for forty-five years. But I have done many fleshly things during that time. The Holy Spirit has been my constant companion. Yet I've often followed the flesh instead of the Spirit.

We all do. Because no one is perfect.

If I follow the flesh, I am condemned. Not by Christ, but by myself. When I do something bad, I tell myself I don't deserve to go to heaven because I'm such a horrible sinner.

God will never condemn you. But He will convict your heart. The Holy Spirit inside you whispers that what you did isn't good, that your behavior needs to change. And that can happen … if you stop thinking about the wrong things.

When we live by the flesh, we are afraid, because we know our sins deserve to be punished. When we live by the Spirit, Christ saves us and the Holy Spirit lead us away from sin. When we live by the Spirit, there is no fear.

The flesh constantly lures us to do things we shouldn't and then leads us into fear and condemnation. For those who believe in Jesus, there is no law to break. We can do anything freely. But the Spirit of God who lives in us has no desire to do those things that hurt others or break God's heart.

When you were a child and your mom told you not to do something, didn't that make you want to do it even more? Well, God says, "Feel free to do as you please! Because I sent Jesus to break the power of sin." As the apostle Paul says (Romans 6:15), why would we go back to following sinful desires when that power has been broken by Christ? We no longer have to be driven by the flesh. We can do the spiritual things God called us to because we have the freedom to follow Him.

We all have both spirits living within us. We sometimes choose to follow the flesh because we forget that we are free from living that way. We are free from those powers now. So we should look and act differently than the rest of the world.

I live in a sin-filled world, but I have the Spirit of Christ living in me. So the things of this world should no longer matter to me. Can I live that way consistently? I'd like to think that I can. But some days are more difficult than others.

If you believe in Jesus Christ, the Spirit of God lives inside you. Jesus will get you into heaven because of what He did, not anything you've done or can do. He loves you. If you meditate on what He has done for you, your mind and heart will have tremendous peace, joy, and comfort. And you will be able to cooperate with the Spirit.

What's on Your Mind?

When I open my Facebook app, it asks, "What's on your mind?" That's a good question to ask yourself throughout the day. Are you thinking the true thoughts that God's Spirit puts into your head? If not, take steps to reprogram your mind. And don't forget to ask God to help you. He will!

Chapter 3

Know You Have an Enemy

*W*hen I was eight years old and living my best life, I decided to get baptized. Not long after that, feelings of shame, condemnation, and unworthiness entered my life.

The enemy of our souls wants to put us in chains and bondage. The devil wants us to feel alone and helpless.

Setting the Scene

In the first story of the Bible, we are introduced to Adam, Eve, and the serpent. When God created the world, on the sixth day He created a man. The man was alone, and God said this was not good. So God brought the animals He had created to Adam and allowed him to name them, but no animal was found that was able to be an appropriate helper for the man.

God put Adam into a deep sleep and formed a woman from one of his ribs. When the man saw her, he said, "This is perfect! She will make me complete." Verse 25 says the man and the woman were naked, but they felt no shame.

Life was good! A man and a woman have trees to eat from and animals to tend the ground. They walk and talk with God all the time, no guilt or condemnation.

Can you imagine yourself in this scene? You have fresh water, delicious food, lush grass, beautiful oak trees and fruit trees, gorgeous sunrises and sunsets, twinkling stars, crickets, fireflies. Your body is perfect (however you picture that), and your man is perfect.

You wake up to a sky painted in pinks, blues, and corals. Colorful hummingbirds fly around you. A cool breeze blowing from the northwest moves your hair around. Your perfect man stands beside you, naked, his arms around your waist. You can feel his breath on your neck. God is with both of you, the composer of this moment.

What could be better than that?

I had a moment similar to that recently. My husband and I enjoy walking around our home in the evenings, especially when fall is about to begin and there is a cool breeze in the air. At one point he stopped and wrapped his arms around me. We were fully clothed, of course. I draped my arms around his neck and gave him a tender kiss.

I wanted to savor that moment. I thanked God for my husband and prayed that He would let me keep that image forever etched in my mind.

I know that someday one of us will become feeble and no longer able to stand. At some point, one of us will leave this earth. Death is part of life, and I never want to forget these special moments or become complacent about them.

But when I focus on my fear of the future, I don't drink in these moments as much as I could. I can't just enjoy the moment for what it is, a chance to live out the ideal I read about in Genesis 2:25.

Why? Because the story continues. Let's look at Genesis chapter 3.

The Enemy Enters

In Genesis 3:1, we are introduced to the serpent. This creature was the devil in fleshly form. He wasn't about to let Adam and Eve enjoy their happily ever after—not without a fight.

The serpent had purely evil intent. He was miserable, and misery always wants company.

Most theological scholars reference Ezekiel 28 to describe the fall of the angel Lucifer, the creature the devil was originally. Let's look at those passages.

> *Son of man, raise a lamentation over the king of Tyre, and say to him, thus says the Lord God:*
> *"You were the signet of perfection, full of wisdom and*

perfect in beauty. You were in Eden, the garden of God; every
precious stone was your covering, sardius, topaz, and diamond,
beryl, onyx, and jasper, sapphire, emerald, and carbuncle; and
crafted in gold were your settings and your engravings. On
the day that you were created they were prepared. You were
an anointed guardian cherub. I placed you; you were on the
holy mountain of God; in the midst of the stones of fire you
walked. You were blameless in your ways from the day you
were created, till unrighteousness was found in you. ... Your
heart was proud because of your beauty; you corrupted your
wisdom for the sake of your splendor. I cast you to the ground;
I exposed you before kings, to feast their eyes on you.
~Ezekiel 28:12–15, 17 ESV

Lucifer was once an angel, and he was perfect. But because of pride in his own beauty, he fell. God put him in the garden of Eden and made him crawl on his belly. And ever since then, humans have been trying to fight him off.

Slap the Enemy

When I was in middle school my family moved to a small town. Not long after, a boy I didn't know came to my home. He made small talk with me for a bit, and then he asked if he could kiss me. I had no interest in this guy, so I told him no.

A couple of days later, a girl approached me at school and asked if I'd tried to kiss her best friend's boyfriend. I denied it, but she didn't believe me.

I could not figure out why she would even think that. Then I realized the boy must have been trying to start something. I don't know why. All I knew was that two girls I barely knew wanted to fight me. I was afraid. I had never been in a fight. I didn't know what to do. I didn't have many friends to support me since I was new in town.

For PE, we all went into the locker room to change before class and then returned to the locker room after. We had a male coach, and he never went into the girls' locker room.

The school grapevine told me these two girls were planning to attack me. Sure enough, when I walked into the locker room, the one who'd accused me earlier was standing there, waiting for me.

She asked, "Why have you been trying to get with my best friend's boyfriend?"

When I told her I wasn't, she slapped me across the face.

I don't know what came over me, but I got so angry I started pounding my fist into her head. I couldn't stop! I just kept punching until she was on the ground trying to pull herself up by my hair.

Someone finally separated us. I gradually calmed down as we all walked outside. I kept my mouth shut so the coach wouldn't know what had happened. I didn't want to get suspended for fighting. But I couldn't stop thinking about it. Why did I have to fight those two girls when I was just trying to do life and not bother anyone?

When we finished jogging around the track, we headed back to the locker room. The girl's best friend glared at me, and I knew I was going to face her wrath again.

She threw a punch at me but missed. This time I did more pushing and prodding than pounding and punching. I didn't have that slap in the face to incite my anger, so it was probably more of an even fight.

From that day forward, nobody messed with me.

Why am I sharing this story? I have a couple of points I want to make about it.

I had an enemy, and I didn't even know it. That boy came by my house subtly, apparently just wanting to chat.

At first, I was scared because I'd never been in a fight before, and I didn't know how to stand up for myself. But once I realized I did have it in me, I wasn't as timid. And after that, people didn't mess with me because they saw I would stand up for myself.

This week something similar happened to me, but not with flesh and blood. Some thoughts subtly entered my mind that I *know* were not from God. Those thoughts tried to tell me terrible things about who I am and who I'm not. *I'm not worthy enough to write a book that might help other people, and I might as well accept that.*

I was under this constant, relentless attack for at least twenty-four hours. Fear welled up inside me. I started to believe the lies.

I walked into the locker room of my mind and got slapped by the devil.

When I realized what was going on, I punched that thought down using the name of Jesus Christ. And you know what happened?

It left me.

My mind was wiped clean.

The devil knows us well. He knows how to get under our skin. What will make us feel like we're not good enough. He will attack us repeatedly to stop us from doing the things God has called us to.

But what if he knew you wouldn't stand for his lies? What if he knew you could whip him? Sooner or later, he'll stop messing with you!

Are you going to let the devil enter your mind whenever he wants and control your thoughts? Or are you going to stand up for yourself and fight for your freedom?

The devil will not mess with somebody he has been unable to defeat!

We have some choices to make. We can go through life hoping the devil doesn't bother us, or we can be alert and watch out for him.

Good vs. Evil

Fred Flintstone, Tom the cartoon cat, Cronk in the *Emperor's New Groove*, Homer Simpson, and Pluto. What do they all have in common?

All these characters have dealt with two voices running simultaneously in their heads. The devil on one shoulder and an angel on the other.

The angel (usually standing on the character's right shoulder) looks like the character but has white wings and maybe a white robe. On the opposite shoulder stands a depiction of the character dressed in red, with horns on its head and a pitchfork.

These images may be funny in a cartoon. But we all have two forces speaking to us and trying to convince us to follow them.

How do you know which voice to follow? It's not always an obvious choice. But there are some filters we can run it through to help us decide.

Following the Wrong Voice

When I was eight or nine, I attended Bible studies with my parents. I wanted to go because there was always a group of kids I could play with while Mom and Dad and their church friends studied the Bible.

One time there was only me and one other girl. As we played games downstairs, she asked me to do something I had never done before. Something that made me feel seriously uncomfortable. But I wanted to be friends with this girl, so I did what she asked me to.

My inner voice told me what I was doing was wrong because I didn't want anybody to know I was doing it.

Afterward, I immediately felt ashamed.

I didn't tell my parents until I was much older.

I wish I would have listened to my inner voice that day and followed the angel me instead of the devil me. The enemy won that day, and he continues to try to use that incident. That one moment in my life has caused me numerous issues.

Do you have memories that make you feel ashamed? Moments you wish you could turn back the clock to and change? I think most people do.

When I was eighteen, I got pregnant. And I made the choice to have an abortion.

I knew instinctively it was wrong. And I had several opportunities to walk away from it.

The main reason I had the abortion was selfishness. I was a teenager and didn't want to raise a child. I also didn't want to tell my parents I was pregnant.

A good friend of mine knew I was planning to have the abortion. On the morning of August 4, she went to my dad's office and told him. When he asked me about it, I had the perfect opportunity to stop the abortion process. But instead, I lied. I told my father a friend of mine was pregnant, and I was going with her to support her. He wasn't happy about that, but it got him off my back

The next day, I got up early and drove an hour to the clinic. Plenty of time to listen to that angel voice and change my mind. I chose not to.

To this day I have deep regrets. The enemy won that battle. He got to me and took me all the way there. I wish I had listened to the other voice.

But I didn't.

Now What?

What happens when we listen to that devil side and the enemy wins? How do we move forward after making a horrible decision?

We turn to God. He can forgive, even when we cannot forgive ourselves. Isaiah 30 brings me tremendous comfort.

This is what the Sovereign Lord,
the Holy One of Israel, says:
"Only in returning to me
and resting in me will you be saved.
In quietness and confidence is your strength.
But you would have none of it." ...
So the Lord must wait for you to come to him
so he can show you his love and compassion.
For the Lord is a faithful God.
Blessed are those who wait for his help.
O people of Zion, who live in Jerusalem,
you will weep no more.
He will be gracious if you ask for help.
He will surely respond to the sound of your cries.
Though the Lord gave you adversity for food
and suffering for drink,
he will still be with you to teach you.
You will see your teacher with your own eyes.
Your own ears will hear him.
Right behind you a voice will say,

"This is the way you should go,"
whether to the right or to the left.

~Isaiah 30: 15, 18–21

When we sin and fall short of God's glorious standard for us, we can turn back to Him. We can be forgiven. He will be with you. And your ears will hear Him. He will be right behind you, telling you which way you should go.

Build a Wall of Protection

Nehemiah built a wall to protect a city. He did this because he recognized that thieves could come in and destroy. But Nehemiah had an enemy who kept trying to stop the wall from being built.

We need to build a wall against our enemy too. He is everywhere and can attack any place and any time. He will taunt you relentlessly, reminding you about your past sins and how you've failed to overcome them.

Nehemiah felt compassion for the people of Jerusalem and believed they were important enough to protect.

You deserve to be protected too! This wall won't restrict you. You can still walk out of the gates whenever you want. But it will protect you from harmful things entering in.

There are probably gaps or holes in your wall that need to be patched up. Ask God to show you where the enemy can still sneak in.

It took Nehemiah fifty-two days to rebuild that wall. There are fifty-two weeks in a year. I challenge you to spend one day per week really praying about the gaps in your wall, and then spend one day putting the truth in those holes. Soon you will have a solid, sturdy fortress of protection.

The Enemy Enters Subtly

Here are some of the cracks the enemy has used to come into my life. Maybe you'll recognize them.

- Taking Scripture out of context
- Questioning the value of attending church
- Getting too deeply involved for the wrong reasons

When I remarried, my husband wanted to go to church, but I wasn't ready. I agreed to go because I liked the pastor. That should've been a red flag.

Once we started attending, I realized this church was growing, and I wanted to be a part of the leadership. In a search for significance, I got heavily involved, and being a part of a big church poured into that desire. The enemy used it to make me feel like I was more than God's child because I was so involved. I became prideful, and when I was asked to step down from the ministry, it caused me to think I was now less than. Not just in my own eyes but in God's eyes too.

I didn't think the enemy could get to me at church, but he did, in the places of me that matter most: my heart and my mind. He can even use Scripture (like he did with Jesus in the wilderness).

Discernment is crucial. Does what you hear and read *about* the Bible coincide with the entire Word of God? You'll only be able to know if you spend time reading and studying it on a regular basis.

Be Aware!

They say hindsight is 20/20. We must learn from our experiences. Be on the lookout for the enemy. He is crafty! And he can take on many identities.

Like Loki from the Marvel series, the devil can change his appearance to try to draw you in. Remember, he just wants you to be miserable like he is. Once he manages to isolate you, it will be hard to escape.

My husband and I live near a state park, and we enjoy hiking there. At the trail head there are warnings to watch out for snakes. If we got bit, we'd probably survive. But how much better to be aware and avoid those snakes!

That is my warning for you. Keep a close eye out for the serpent's temptations. More important, keep your focus on the one who can protect you from them and provide a way of escape when he rears his ugly head.

Chapter 4

Figure Out What Is Weighing You Down

I got up early this morning to pray. Before I could start, I needed to do a load of laundry. After putting the clothes into the washing machine, I noticed clutter in the kitchen, so I did a little cleanup. Before I knew it, an hour had gone by, and I never prayed.

I sat down at my laptop, quieted myself, and turned on the computer to type out my prayers. When I opened Word, the first thing I saw was my Christmas list. I needed to get on the internet to start shopping.

It's amazing how easily I can get distracted.

Many things can get in the way of finding our divine design. A few of my own include thinking I know what is best for my life, living an unhealthy lifestyle, comfort, other people, social influence, fear, and making life too complicated. I'll deal with each of these in this chapter.

If you can relate to those struggles, I suggest you pray before you read this chapter. Ask the Holy Spirit to guide you as you read.

Here is a sample prayer:

Heavenly Father, I praise You for Your love and Your guidance. I want to know what is getting in the way from finding my divine design. I'm about to read someone else's story. If there is something in this that should resonate within me, help me see it. If not, help me to disregard it. I want You with me on this journey. In Jesus's name, amen.

I Know What Is Best for My Life

I was raised in church, knowing right from wrong. Yet I didn't trust God, or my parents, to lead my life. If Mom and Dad told me not to do something, their rule fueled something within me to do it anyway. My parents didn't understand me. They didn't know my wants and needs. I had to find them for myself.

When I was fourteen years old, I dated a boy my parents didn't approve of. I even snuck out of the window one night to go hang out with him. The relationship didn't last long. We broke up after about six months.

The next boyfriend I picked was one my parent's thought was better for me. But he tried to get me to do things with him I didn't want to do, so I stopped seeing him.

Mom and Dad weren't so sure about my next boyfriend. During the two years we dated, I lost my virginity and started smoking and drinking. But I still thought I knew what was best for me. Nobody was going to tell me how to live my life.

I am much older and wiser now. I no longer try to disobey my parents or God or purposely go against their authority. I have seen the consequences that come from living a sinful lifestyle. Like the Apostle Paul said, I have not reached perfection yet (Philippians 3:12). But I am more aware of how my desire to control my life gets in the way of finding my divine design.

Self-discipline or the Scale?

I have struggled my entire life with body image and self-esteem. To be honest, I fight the urge even today to let those things define who I am. The devil can be so relentless!

I have tried several types of diets. Even one where I tried not to eat much at all and nearly starved myself to death.

Eventually I found a diet plan that worked for me: Weight Watchers. I have learned to understand how certain foods make me feel. When I eat a cookie, ice cream, or a bunch of chips and dip, I feel miserable—not physically, but mentally, because I know eating that kind of food is going to make me gain weight.

One day, as I was reading Scripture, John chapter 4 stood

out to me like never before. As Jesus was talking to the Samaritan woman, His disciples came back from town. They asked Him if He wanted some food, and Jesus responded, "The food I eat is doing the will of My Father." It hit me that I needed to view food that way too.

When I overindulge, I feel guilty and full of shame. If the scale doesn't tell me what I want, I become discouraged and depressed. But my worth is not in how well I can control what food I put in my mouth or what the scale says. My worth comes from God. I am His child. He loves me.

Time Limitations and Distractions

From the day you were made in your mother's womb (see Psalm 139), your heavenly Father had a divine design in mind just for you. And ever since that day, the enemy has been trying to distract you from it.

A distraction can be anything that gets in the way of you doing what you need to do to live out your divine design. Many distractions are good things done out of balance.

If we focus too much on our own comfort, we won't get off the couch to exercise or communicate with our children. If we concentrate on what we are going to eat, we may become lazy, depressed, or guilty. If we spend all our time working, our relationships will suffer, laundry will pile up, and dirty dishes will overflow in the sink.

Everything requires time.

You keep track of how you spend your money so you don't spend more than you have. You count calories because you don't want to gain weight. Why not plan your time too? I challenge you to sit down and ask God what His divine design is for you. Then close your eyes for five minutes and meditate on this question: *Where do I see myself in ten years?*

Do you want to have peace and joy in all circumstances? Then you need to spend time building a relationship with your heavenly Father.

Do you want to be physically and mentally fit? Then figure out how to accomplish that.

Do you want solid relationships with your children? Make time for them.

Count how much time you spend each week on activities like driving to school, going to work, cleaning the bathroom, cooking supper, watching Netflix, praying, making money, resting, exercising, studying, learning a new skill, playing, organizing, paying bills, grocery shopping, and taking a nap. Are you using the limited time you have doing things that will enable you to live out your divine design?

How much time do you spend doing the things God has called you to? Building those important relationships with God and your spouse, children, grandchildren, and friends?

One day I felt a still, small voice whisper in my ear, "Tithe your time." According to Malachi 3:10–12, a tithe is 10 percent. It can mean a tenth of your money or your time. The Scriptures declare that if we bring our tithes to God, He will open the windows of heaven for us and pour out a blessing so great we won't have enough room to take it all in.

While I was working on my master's degree, I had many papers due at once. I felt overwhelmed. I sensed the Holy Spirit leading me to take a break from schoolwork on Sundays and give that day to God. Though the idea frightened me, the message was so strong I had to go for it.

God blessed my decision. I received a perfect score on the next few papers I turned in. I'd never made those kinds of grades!

What do you feel led by the Spirit to do when it comes to your time? It may be taking ten minutes a day to read God's Word and have a conversation with Him. Or it could be starting a prayer journal.

The most important thing you can do with your time is to seek the Lord's divine design for you. Ask Him what that design is, then listen to His answer. When He whispers something to you, write it down, ponder it, then do it, without letting any distractions keep you from it.

God made you, and He has a divine design for you. He has been speaking to you about it since the day you were born. Pausing to seek Him and listen will be well worth your time!

Comfort

Comfort can be viewed from two perspectives. One is what you feel while sitting in a cozy chair curled up with a soft blanket. The other is how you feel about where you are in life. Both comforts can keep you from pursuing your divine design.

In *The Miracle Morning for Writers*, author Hal Elrod suggests making time to do things that are important to you by getting up an hour earlier than normal. Some days I have a hard time getting up early to pray, write, or read because my bed is so comfortable. But when I do, I enjoy those quiet, peaceful times with minimal distractions. And I find I have more energy throughout the day. And I accomplish goals—like writing this book.

How badly do you want peace, hope, and joy? Enough to start getting up early to pray?

What kind of comforts are you willing to give up pursuing your divine design?

Other People

Sometimes family and friends can get in the way of pursuing our divine design. If God is calling you to something that those close to you don't understand, you have to move forward anyway.

On the other hand, there are some situations where family and friends can help push us toward our divine design ... or prevent us from doing something stupid. We need discernment when it comes to these matters. Ask the Holy Spirit for guidance. If God is in it, you will find peace.

Be careful who you share your passions with. Choose people who will encourage you.

When I felt led to go back to school and earn my master's degree, I wanted to go to Florida State University. That would require that I quit my job. My husband was not thrilled. After some prompting by the Holy Spirit, I quit my job and went back to school. God opened doors for me and provided for our needs in mighty ways. My husband finally concluded that God was in this situation.

My husband could have stopped me from pursuing my divine

design if I hadn't persisted and if God hadn't shown up in the way He did.

The World

What does society say is okay, and though you don't agree, you go along with it anyway? Do you feel led to stand up for something, but you don't for fear of what other people might think? You may be allowing the world to squash your divine design.

Fear

Eve had doubts that God was holding out on her, so she chose to do her own thing. Fear of missing out drove her to do things her own way.

Fear also drives me to get stuck when I have an important choice to make. I'm afraid if I go down the wrong road, God will no longer be with me. Or at the very least I'll be wasting my time. I fear what people will think of me or say about me. I fear I won't fit in. I fear I will lose relationships with the people I love.

We cannot allow fear to stop us from pursuing our divine design. God is with us, so we have nothing to fear!

Making it Too Complicated

I am always looking for the next big thing I need to do, or what sin I need to overcome to find my divine design. But it's not that complicated. The way to find your divine design is to just talk to God, believe in Jesus Christ, and listen to and cooperate with the Holy Spirit.

Clean Your Room!

Several things can stand in the way of pursuing your divine design. But God is always with you, helping you see and avoid those distractions.

When my two daughters were growing up, I asked them every week to clean their rooms. They'd do it, but within a couple of days, the rooms would be just as messy as before.

That's how it is with the things that weigh us down.

Every week we need to check ourselves and consider what things are standing in our way, pray about them, and ask God to help us overcome them.

Chapter 5

Remember Who You Are

I sat at the kitchen counter, staring at the dirty plates, pots, and pans. I'd done it again. Yesterday I starved myself. Today I overate. *Why can I not break free from this issue?*

Ever since I was little, I have struggled with my body image. According to the BMI scale, I have been obese, and I have fallen in the normal range. One year I took on a weight-loss challenge at work and lost almost twenty pounds. I was so thin, my body looked saggy and bony.

I thought I would love myself after losing all that weight. I didn't.

As soon as the weight-loss challenge ended, I started binging on junk food and sweets like I hadn't eaten in months. I gained weight a little bit at a time until I was up ten pounds. I felt okay at that weight. But I knew if I didn't stop eating all the junk, I'd get right back to square one. And summer was just around the corner.

I struggled for three months to keep the weight off.

When Fall began, I decided to take back control of my life. I began to journal my food intake and weigh myself once a week. In the first two weeks, I lost three pounds. So far, so good.

The following week I ate whatever I wanted but did not overindulge. At the end of week three, I weighed the same. Life was good.

I ate healthy during the week and pigged out on the weekend, keeping my weight the same. A good place to be!

At the beginning of week four, I stepped onto the scale and found I'd gained two pounds. I fell into a terrible depression and started hating myself again.

What a crazy way to live! I'm constantly either depriving myself or stuffing myself. Whenever I look in the mirror, I find something to complain about. After polishing off an entire bag of chips, guilt sets in. I knew when I grabbed that snack out of the pantry that I shouldn't eat it, but I did anyway.

It's a vicious cycle.

Knowing I needed God's help to get off this hamster wheel, I began a prayer journal.

September 6

Dear heavenly Father, I thank You for the good news of Jesus Christ and what He did for me on the cross. I praise You that because of Him I will never be thirsty again.

Some days I forget that I'm loved by the King of all kings! Some days I forget that You are my satisfaction and You've given me all that I need. Help me remember these truths today, Father. Please show me where I'm trying to fill up my water jar with things of this world.

September 7

It's crazy how quickly I forget the truths You've shown me. You know me, Lord. You created me and led me into Your divine design for me. Teach me. Help me to hear You loud and clear.

September 11

I praise You for filling me. Help me remember today that I am Your daughter. I am the woman who has touched the hem of Your robe. My water jar is full and laid at Your feet. You are my shepherd, and You have given me all I need.

Sin has lost its control over me. I have what it takes because You live within me.

September 12

I need Your love, forgiveness, and counsel. I cannot seem to make it through a day without turning to some sort of food for comfort, even though I know that's what I'm about to do before I do it. I ask You to help me meditate on truth. I forget Your truths so easily. I think meditation is the key to a lot of my issues.

The next day I had an ophthalmologist appointment and had my eyes dilated. When I got home, I tried to read Scripture instead of turning to food. But I couldn't see clearly. So I went grocery shopping, picked up fried chicken on the way home, and bought candy corn from Walmart.

After overindulging with two pieces of chicken, mashed potatoes, a buttered biscuit, and two heaping handfuls of candy, I laid down on the couch to watch television. I instantly felt the urge to get up and go to the pantry for more food. I made it an hour before I pigged out on chips, dip, and ice cream.

The next morning, I woke up with major condemnation. I was so mad at myself. And totally frustrated.

Yet again I turned to my gracious, forgiving heavenly Father in prayer.

While I was praying, my husband crouched down beside me and said, "My beautiful, lovely bride!"

I did not believe his words.

After he left the room, I wrote in my journal.

I'm under attack, God. The arrows are coming fast!

Where is the balance? Have You shown me and I'm missing it? Lord, what do You want for me?

I heard His voice respond with one word. *Peace.*

I didn't want to be conformed by this world. But sometimes I felt like it was too late.

"Help me, Lord," I prayed out loud. "Forgive me yet again. Please fill in the gaps, God!"

I prayed that same prayer repeatedly over the next couple of weeks. And I kept hearing that still, small voice say, *Remember who you are.* That phrase made me think of the popular Disney movie *The Lion King.* As I sat in my prayer closet one day, I searched YouTube for the video clip that contained the phrase.

Simba is doubting his identity. So Rafiki leads him to a pool of water and encourages him to look into it

Simba peers at his reflection and scoffs.

Rafiki tells him to look closer. When Simba looks again, he sees his image turn into his father's face.

The Holy Spirit spoke to me through the voice of Rafiki. "You see? He lives in you!"

In the scene, Simba's father, Mufasa, shows up. As I watched, I heard the voice of God say to me, "Elizabeth, you have forgotten who you are, so you have forgotten Me. Look inside yourself. You are more than what you have become. You must take your place in this world. Remember who you are: My precious daughter."

Crying, I raised my hands to the one who made me. Astonished and amazed, I praised the Lord who lives in me.

He lives in you too! He's saying to you right now, "You are My child, and you need to take your place in the world. You are above what the world has to offer because I live in you!"

As I basked in the joy that came over me, a song came to my mind. "He Lives in You" by Lebo M. I quickly went to YouTube to find the recording. I sang the lyrics over and over, acknowledging that no mountain could be too big if I had faith because Jesus lives in me and watches over me. In the reflection of the water of truth, I saw His reflection in me.

I then felt led to Scripture. Could there be a passage that would back up what I felt in my spirit?

I went back to a page in my journal where I had written down some verses from Romans chapter 8.

verse 1: No condemnation for those who belong to Christ Jesus.

verse 3: Sin has no control over you.

verse 9: You are controlled by the Spirit.

verse 10: Christ lives within you. Even though your body will die because of sin, the Spirit gives you life because you have been made right with God.

verse 11: The Spirit of God, who raised Jesus from the dead, lives in you! And just as God raised Jesus from the dead, He will give life to your mortal body by this same Spirit living within you.

After reading those passages, I praised the Lord for His unfailing love and forgiveness. I also praised Him for being in the details of my life and for speaking truth to me about who I am.

Five months after I had this spiritual experience with the Lord, I was invited to give a talk at my church on James chapter 1. I prayed about it and read the Scripture passage several times. Each time, I could not get that phrase, "Remember who you are," out of my mind.

James chapter 1 is famous because of the author's search for wisdom. I ask God for wisdom all the time because I want to get things right in my life. I've gotten so many things wrong, and I'm tired of running the rat race and getting nowhere.

In preparation for my talk, I jotted down four pages of notes about what a religious person would tell you to do. But it didn't seem right, because I kept hearing in my head, *Remember who you are.*

James says this world will bring troubles. And boy, was he right. Troubles are rampant these days. Everyone experiences them.

James tells us we should be *happy* when we have troubles because they build our faith. When we come to the end of ourselves, we have no choice but to put our hope in God.

Troubles should make us give up, let go, and let God! The harder the trouble, the more likely we are to look to our Maker, the one who can help us through it.

As I repeatedly read through James chapter 1, I realized that I needed to remember who I am when it comes to body image and other things as well.

I encourage you to read this chapter from Scripture through the filter of the phrase, "Remember who you are."

When trouble comes, remember who you are. And remember who God is. If you need wisdom, ask Him, and He will give it to you. If you are poor, feeling life fade away, enduring testing, tempted, listening to negative things others say or that you're saying to yourself, remember who you are.

You are God's child. He lives in you. You are more than a conqueror in Jesus Christ.

As His child, you can do what God wants you to do: love others and love yourself.

Chapter 6

Know How Much God Loves You

Our view of God's love begins by the way we are loved by our parents. Being raised in a Christian home, I heard "God loves you" a lot, but I didn't understand what that meant. I knew my parents loved me. Yet I felt more loved by them when I got their attention through a performance of some kind. I figured God must love the same way.

To me, God lived high in the clouds and constantly told me what I could and could not do. When I chose the wrong action, I felt ashamed.

I constantly tried to figure out whether God loved me and if He was pleased with me. I believed that the more I performed for Him, the more He would accept me and love me. I didn't understand that God loves me no matter what I do.

I thought He set up rules to make me miserable. I didn't realize those rules were in place *because* He loved me.

When I was thirty-two years old, some situations in my life forced me to take a hard look at myself and my view of God. Who was He? Why did He create me? What was the deal with sin? What was Christ's role? What was the Holy Spirit?

It occurred to me that my faith in God was based solely on my parents' testimony and experiences. And that would no longer keep me afloat.

How I Got My View of God

The pastor of the church my husband and I attended was all about personal development and reading nonfiction books. He also believed strongly in journaling. He gave me a yellow legal pad and told me to write down the following: *God is most glorified in me when I am most satisfied with Him.* I didn't know it at the time, but I was about to begin a long journey of getting to know God on a more personal level.

When I started on this journey, I was unsure of where to begin. I had a lot of questions for God, but I didn't know what to do about them. The pastor suggested I read one of the short books in the New Testament repeatedly while praying and taking notes.

I started with Ephesians. I wrote down my thoughts and questions in the journal and talked to God about them. I was honest with my questions. I figured the only way I was going to find what I was looking for was by being honest with myself and with Him.

My first questions were: *Why would God create me for His purpose? What is God's purpose? What's in it for me?*

Ephesians 1:12 told me to praise God. *Why? Was He lonely? I guess so. Why else would He create human beings?*

I concluded that I could not fully understand why. If I did, God would not be bigger than me.

God knew that human beings would sin when He created them. Yet He gave us the free will to choose life or death.

There is no joy in making someone love me or want to spend time with me. If someone is pursuing me, I feel loved and wanted. In the same way, God wants us to choose Him, not be forced to do so.

I still ask God questions today. If I come to a passage in scripture I do not understand or if something in life has me puzzled, I ask God about it. I want to know and live my life understanding God's perfect love for me.

Here are some ways you can start to build your knowledge of God and His love for you.

Through Scripture

When you open the Bible, you'll see God's love through the pages. You'll see it when He parted the sea for the Israelites, rescued Daniel from the lions' den, stood in the fire with Shadrach,

Meshach, and Abednego, and spoke to Moses. Most importantly, you see it when He sent His Son to die for your sins.

Through Your Love Language

Gary Chapman, a family counselor, became curious about what caused couples to divorce and what could be done to rectify the problem. He conducted research on how people love and like to be loved. He published his findings in his book *The Five Love Languages*, which identifies five common ways to express and receive love: words of affirmation, acts of service, physical touch, gifts, and quality time. The book was so popular, Chapman wrote ten more books in the series.

In his books, Chapman suggests that we each have two dominant love languages. We can feel love through all of them, but there are usually two that speak to us the most.

My love languages are personal touch and gifts. I feel most loved when my husband buys me something unexpected or when he holds my hand, or we snuggle together on the couch.

My husband's love languages are personal touch and acts of service. He shows me his love by holding my hand and by doing things around the house because that's how he wants to be loved.

Because one of my dominant love languages is gifts, I know God loves me because He has provided many gifts to me. My husband, children, grandchildren, parents, extended family. My home, my job, my dogs. Sunsets, sunrises, wind, the beach, the Bible. My list could go on and on.

Because personal touch is my other dominant love language, I enjoy lying out in the sun, feeling the heat on my body—especially when a cool breeze from the north blows my hair around. I see these as God's personal touches. When I get a hug from my grandson, daughter, or husband, I view these as personal touches from God too.

Through Christ

The most personal way I know God loves me is because of what He did to free me: Jesus Christ. My favorite Bible verse is

John 3:16: "For God so *loved* the world, that he *gave* his only Son, that whoever believes in him should not perish but have eternal life" (ESV, emphasis mine).

Through the Holy Spirit

Whenever I'm struggling with something I read in the Bible, I have a moment with the Lord about it, and that makes all the difference in understanding God's love for me. That's the work of the Holy Spirit.

There are other ways the Holy Spirit speaks to me. For example, one day, my grandson was playing with my phone. The next day, when I opened my music app, it pulled up the last song he had listened to: "It Was Always You" by Maroon 5. I hadn't heard that song in a long time.

As I listened to it, the lyrics spoke to me in a profound way. I realized that I had been trying to separate God from Jesus Christ. But when God came to earth in human form, He *was* Jesus. It was always Him. God never left Jesus.

I believed the Holy Spirit was speaking to me through the words of the song. God wanted to bring me back to Him. He wanted the same kind of relationship with me that He had with Jesus.

Whenever I think of Jesus, I think of being in love—Jesus reaching out His hand and saving me. Yet when I think of God, I tend to think about judgment and condemnation. I had forgotten that God and Jesus are the same—they live within each other.

When Jesus came to earth, He was God in human form. When Jesus died on the cross for my sins, God did too! That's the mystery of the Trinity. God, Jesus Christ, and the Holy Spirit are one.

In John chapter 14, Philip said to Jesus,

> *"Lord, show us the Father, and we will be satisfied."*
> *Jesus replied, "Have I been with you all this time, Philip, and yet you still don't know who I am? Anyone who has seen me has seen the Father! So why are you asking me to show him to you? Don't you believe that I am in the*

Father and the Father is in me? The words I speak are not my own, but my Father who lives in me does his work through me. Just believe that I am in the Father and the Father is in me. Or at least believe because of the work you have seen me do."

~John 14;8–11

John 1:1 says, "In the beginning the Word already existed. The Word was with God, and the Word was God."

In Romans 9:5, Paul tells his Jewish brothers and sisters that Abraham, Isaac, and Jacob are their ancestors and "Christ himself was an Israelite as far as his human nature is concerned. And he is God, the one who rules over everything and is worthy of eternal praise! Amen."

The Maroon 5 song made me so thankful that when God made me, He gave me free will. He knew there would be times when I would try to run away from Him, when the devil and his demonic forces would try to pull me away from Him.

From the beginning, God had already decided He was going to bring us back to Him—not because of anything we were going to do or not do but because of His glorious plan. Jesus is God, and God is Jesus.

In addition to the Maroon 5 song "It Was Always You," I encourage you to listen to "Higher Love," written by Steve Winwood and Will Jennings. They are sure to make your spirit soar!

He Loves You

God wants you to know that He loves you, unconditionally and unconventionally.

God loves you perfectly. He created you. He knows you fully and He accepts you fully. He loves you so much that He gave you freedom to choose His love, to believe in His love, and to follow His love. No one will make you love Him—not even Him.

God will let you live on your own without His love. He will not force you to stay in His love. He has done all He can do for you. It is your choice to live in His love or not to.

43

But God's love is always available to you. All you have to do is accept, trust, and follow.

What has God done to prove His love?

1. He made you.
2. He gave you freedom to choose what kind of life you want to live.
3. In Christ He provided a sacrifice for your sins for all time.
4. He places desires within you that please the Holy Spirit.
5. He gave you the Holy Spirit to guide you.
6. He is always calling you to a higher love.

Accept His Love for You

Once you decide to accept God's love, He will open His loving arms and embrace you with a love you have never experienced before.

If you don't know how to accept His love, you can start with this prayer:

> *Dear God, I want to accept Your love for me. I would like to know why You created me. I desire to know and feel Your unconditional love for me. Please teach me about Your Son, Jesus. Guide me into the truth about You and Your love for me. Prove to me that You are real and that You love me unconditionally. Help me to see how You have been loving me but I've missed it. Open my eyes to Your love. Embrace me with Your love. I want to know You more. I want to learn more about You, but I don't know where to begin. Guide me to You and Your love. Rescue me with Your love. Draw me to Your higher love. Amen.*

Chapter 7

Sit at Jesus feet!

My dear Martha, you are worried and upset over all these details! There is only one thing worth being concerned about. Mary has discovered it, and it will not be taken away from her.

~Luke 10:41, 42 NLT

I stay busy, and I'm always concerned about many things. Yep, I tend to be more of a Martha than a Mary. But I strive to be like Mary. Siting at Jesus's feet sounds wonderful. Heavenly, even!

Jesus has chosen me when I've felt left out, danced with me when I needed cheering up, been my water when I was dry, and rescued me every time I got myself in a jam. I hope as you read these short stories that you'll think about some of your own similar experiences and recognize how He has shown Himself to you. Come, let's sit at His feet together.

He Chose Me

It seems like I'm always looking for the next great thing, the next high, the next career. I often feel like I'm not measuring up or I'm not doing what I'm supposed to be doing with my life.

A few years ago, when I worked at a high school and was a physical education teacher, I also sponsored the Fellowship of Christian Athletes (FCA). A woman came to speak to the FCA students. Her story stood out to me because she shared that she had plans to become an Olympian boxer, but it didn't work out. Instead, she was placed in a different position, helping others become boxers and sharing her faith with them. She mentioned feeling a completeness inside. I wanted to feel that.

I sat in a corner contemplating my incompleteness, with kids all around me bumping the volleyball in the air, playing basketball, and walking around the gym. With all this movement going on, I started thinking about how Jesus is called the cornerstone. I pictured Him standing in the corner across the room and then walking toward me. He pushed basketballs, kids, and volleyballs out of the way to get to me.

This mental vision hit me deeply. Jesus makes me complete. I don't need a job to make me feel complete. I just need Christ.

That vision led me to write this poem. Read it slowly, to yourself.

I can see Him standing across the dark, fuzzy, and crowded room.
    I cannot make out what He truly looks like,
    but I know I'm drawn to Him.
       His stature is inviting and calls out to me.
I am paralyzed.

He is scanning the room.
    Suddenly
    His gaze stops at me.
       He walks across the room.
    Is He coming to see me?

Someone goes up to Him and starts talking.
    I begin to doubt.
    He pushes them aside and continues His way
       across the crowded room.
    Another approaches him and
       He does the same.
    His walk is determined and purposeful.

When He is about three feet in front of me,
    A crowd of dancers comes between us.

I lose His gaze.
  I put my head down in despair.
I have lost all hope.
  But then,
I feel a warm breeze touch my face.
  I look up, and it's Him!
Our eyes meet for the first time.
  I feel as though He can see right through me.
I am frozen.

He stretches out His hand
      and speaks the words I long to hear:
      Shall we dance?

He Leads Me

Life is not a line dance. But sometimes I wish it was.

Growing up, I used to love watching musicals. I've always had a love for music. I enjoyed dancing for my parents in our living room. You could put on any song, and I'd find a reason to dance to it.

As I reached middle-school age, I decided that dancing in front of people was embarrassing. Especially if you didn't know what you were doing. Freestyle dancing seemed quite scary after I reached a certain age. As I got older it became more intimidating. Until I learned about line dancing.

Line dancing involves learning certain steps and then putting those steps to music. Easy—once you learn how. And others are messing up along with me, so it's not such a big deal.

What's bad about line dancing, or any kind of choreographed dance put to music, is that it changes the way you listen to that music. Once you learn a dance to a particular song, whenever you hear that song, you want to do that dance. I can't dance freely to the electric slide, for example, because I've wired my brain to do that choreographed electric slide line dance.

The same thing happens with religion. Every denomination gives us certain steps we have to take. Each church has its own choreographed dances with Jesus. I've been to several types of churches throughout my life. I could enter just about any Christian denomination and quickly be able to pick up the dance steps.

But that doesn't truly satisfy me.

Like any Christian, I believe that Jesus died on the cross for my sins. I want Him to tell me the steps to take to make life better, easier, more comfortable, less embarrassing, and more controlled. I want to go to Jesus and take His hand and lead Him to the dance floor. I want to do a line dance with Him. I want to know the steps ahead: when to turn left, when to stomp my feet, when to shuffle, and when to do a do-si-do.

But as I have been learning how to dance with Jesus, I've come to realize something.

Jesus is not a line dancer.

We don't go get Jesus from across the crowded room and bring Him to the dance floor to teach Him the dance. Jesus comes and gets us. He chooses us. We must decide for ourselves to take His hand. Once we do, we want Him to teach us the steps. He does that—but often not the way we think He would.

We must let Jesus lead. We need to leave our worries and cares behind, and when He says, "Come, follow Me," we take His hand and trust His lead. Sometimes it may come from a certain religion or church. But we have to make sure we're following Jesus's lead, not men.

Every now and again, I can convince my husband to go to ballroom dance lessons. The last time we went, we learned how to do some turns that go along with the jitterbug. The instructor showed us how to hold hands, stand, move our feet, and do the turns. I had to allow my husband to lead. His body movement and tug of my hand lets me know when to turn under his arm. If I don't know he's going to turn me, it's difficult to make the right moves.

I started loosening my tight grip on his hands so I could feel the slight push in his arms to lead me into the turn. It's a fun dance. But I'm amazed at how aware I need to be of his body language. If I don't feel the turn coming, it's a mess. I step on his toes, and our arms get tangled up. I have to really pay attention.

My husband also has a job to do in this dance. He has to

warn me ahead of time. He can't just do whatever he wants without giving me some kind of push back or pull to or communicate something through his eyes that says a turn is coming. If we don't communicate with our touch, we falter in our dance.

There's something very gentle and moving about dancing with a partner. When you watch a couple dance, you don't normally see them talking to each other about what to do next. No, the communication comes through their senses. It's a purposeful surrender to someone else's will, to find the harmony or rhythm of the other person. It's not easy! But when you submit to this purposeful surrender, the dance becomes so much more fun. It's like riding a roller coaster and anticipating the next turn. You know it's coming. You wait in gleeful expectation. There is no fear because you trust your partner.

I want my dance with Jesus to be like that. I want to purposefully surrender to His will for me. As I wait expectantly, I want to feel His slight tug to turn … the still, small voice.

Today I purposefully surrender my day to Jesus. I feel that slight tug on my hand, I see the look in His eyes, and I know a fun twirl is right around the corner.

He Forgives Me

There are several things in my life that I'm ashamed of. When these things crop up in my mind, they can stall me on my path to freedom in Christ. The enemy enjoys reminding me of my past so he can keep me worrying about it.

When I was younger, some things that made me feel ashamed were sexual. The devil likes to remind me of them at the worst times, like when I'm around my husband, friends, or family. I did those things when I was little, when I was in my teens and twenties.

When we're little, we don't really understand our bodies. So we experience things out of curiosity. Like figuring out how different foods taste.

When I was a teen, I was promiscuous with boys. I knew I shouldn't have sex with them, but I did. I also watched pornography at times. I hoped that once I grew up, those thoughts would leave, but they didn't. Even after I was married, I couldn't seem to shake these images from my mind.

Those images still enter my mind today. It's one of the ways the devil attempts to attack me and make me feel shameful and dirty. He tries to convince me to believe that if people really knew the thoughts that enter my mind, they wouldn't love me or even like me anymore.

I was talking to a friend about this one day, and she asked me, "Have you forgiven yourself for these things?" I'd never really thought about that. I had asked others to forgive me, people I had hurt over the years by my behavior and promiscuity. But I hadn't forgiven myself.

I knew Jesus had forgiven me, but I couldn't forgive myself. I know this is no longer who I am. But the devil is relentless.

I had to come to the cross of Christ and remember that anything I repented of is forgiven and obliterated by the blood of Christ. Everything is gone! I am a new creation in Christ. What Jesus did at the cross covers me. And it covers you too.

Put down this book right now and grab a pen and a piece of paper. At the top of the page, write your name. Underneath that, write down the things in your life that you think are getting between you and God. Then put God's name at the bottom of the list.

Now write your name at the top again. Draw the cross of Christ over all those things the devil keeps reminding you of. Then put God's name at the bottom again.

You no longer have to carry those things with you. Jesus Christ took care of them. They are wiped out. Gone. Destroyed. Because of what Christ did at the cross for you, you don't have to look at them, deal with them, or be reminded of them anymore. You are free!

Before Christ

Me

Sexual promiscuity

Watching porn

Abortion

God

After Christ

50

Me

God

Jesus has stepped in and wiped those things away. We can come to God through Jesus Christ and stand before Him without a single fault. We can also view ourselves in His light.

He Softens Me

I once went on a canoe trip with my husband and daughter down the Ecofina Creek. There are beautiful natural springs there. I'd never seen a bubbling spring before.

While we were on the creek, my husband pulled right up to a spring so I could look down into it. The water was so extremely clear it looked like diamonds were popping out of nowhere. Underneath those diamonds it was dark. And the water was slowly bubbling up to the surface. Beautiful! Breathtaking!

I fixated on this spring for a couple of weeks. I woke up in the middle of the night thinking about it. Thought about it whenever I went for a walk.

John chapter 4 tells a story about a woman who goes to a well to try to get some water. She runs into Jesus sitting there, and He asks her for a drink. The woman is shocked. This Jew shouldn't even want to talk to her because of who she is. Jesus says to her, "If you only knew the gift God has for you and who you are speaking to, you would ask me, and I would give you living water."

Her response: "But sir, you don't have a rope or a bucket, and this well is very deep. Where would you get this living water?"

Jesus replies, "Anyone who drinks this water will soon become thirsty again. But those who drink the water I give will never be thirsty again … It becomes a fresh, *bubbling spring* within them, giving them eternal life." (John 4:7–13, emphasis added)

The water Jesus gives is living water, like a bubbling spring. Did you know that the water that comes out of a bubbling spring is pure and drinkable?

Where does the water for the spring come from? Rain! The living water Jesus gives comes into our lives like rain. Sometimes a sprinkle, other times a few drops, other times a bucket all at once.

One sprinkle could be a kiss or a kind word from someone, either friend or foe. A few drops could be a sermon, a good book, or advice from a friend. A bucket could be a painful experience you've come out of, a healing touch, or laughter.

How much rain does it take to become a bubbling spring? In John 7:37–38, Jesus says, "Anyone who is thirsty may come to me! Anyone who believes in me may come and drink! For the Scriptures declare, 'Rivers of living water will flow from his heart.'"

If we believe in Jesus, living water will flow from us. We don't have to *do* anything to get this flow of water. We just need to accept Jesus into our hearts and wait for the rain. If we believe, we will be a bubbling spring—beauty, diamonds, overflow, pure, and fresh.

For rainwater to become a bubbling spring, it must come down to the earth, and the ground must be permeable for it to be absorbed. If the rain hits asphalt, it cannot absorb. Similarly, we must be permeable (or weak) to allow Jesus's rainwater to seep deep down into us. If we are impervious, the living water just evaporates.

Have you ever seen pavement when the sun is beating down on it after a rain? The water doesn't have time to go beyond the surface, and it just looks like steam.

How many times have I received some rain from God and attempted to do too much and then ended up letting out a lot of steam? Got burnt out, angry, and tired.

When we wait patiently, the rain has time to seep in and go beyond the surface. The deeper it goes, the purer it becomes.

Rainwater is full of impurities. Unless we get our water directly from Jesus Christ, it's going to have some impurities in it. Jesus must take it and make it pure, and the only place to do that is deep within the heart. It has to pass through all our imperviousness and into the permeable parts of us.

The impervious parts are the ones that still believe in the lies the serpent has fed us about our past hurts and fears.

I want to be permeable. I long for the Living Water to seep deep down into my heart so I can be beautiful and bubbling from within. I can be pure because Jesus Christ lives within me!

Sometimes the overflow of the bubbling spring is manifested in our lives through tears. Tears can be indications of letting go of all control and allowing the Holy Spirit to cleanse us deep in our hearts.

In the past, temples were built around springs. People were drawn to spring water because it was pure and drinkable. The more we allow the Living Water deep within us, the more people will want to be around us because we are giving off an air about us that they want to share in.

Can we deplete our bubbling spring? Of course. We are human, after all. We must depend on Jesus Christ and the Holy Spirit for more rainwater each day. God promises us more when we are dry. He will guide us continually, restoring our strength. We will be like well-watered gardens, nourished from an every-flowing spring.

He Frees Me

One morning I was sitting on the beach, watching the waves hit the shore, gazing at the sunrise as it clothed the clouds with various hues of light pink, blue, and purple. I thought about that famous story of Jesus walking on the water.

While in a daze of amazement, thanking my heavenly Father for the beautiful morning, I saw a swarm of seagulls moving in a figure-eight pattern. Why were they flying that way?

They seemed to be concerned about something in the ocean. Was it a tasty fish? A scary shark?

A nearby fisherman on the shore began reeling something in. As the line got shorter, I saw that he had captured a seagull with his hook. It flapped about, trying to break free. It nipped at the fisherman, who was hurriedly trying to free it. The other seagulls quickly went their own ways.

I felt such sorrow for this seagull, I couldn't continue watching the horrific scene. I looked away and prayed, *Dear God, please help free that seagull! I don't want to watch it die.*

A woman sitting close by, probably the fisherman's wife, got out of her chair and tried to assist him in freeing the distressed seagull. But to no avail.

I looked away again and prayed some more.

When I turned back, I noticed another man standing with the fisherman. He took the fishing line in one hand and gently lifted the hook out of the seagull. To my relief, the bird didn't drop to the ground. It soared off into the beautiful blue sky, flapping its wings majestically.

I sobbed. *Hallelujah! Praise the Lord! It has been freed! Thank You, Father, for rescuing that seagull!*

This story has stayed with me, I suppose, because I see myself in the characters. You may see yourself in them too.

First, I'm the fisherman. Just standing on the shore of this life, casting my line into the world, hoping I'll catch something I can be proud of or that will feed me.

I'm also the fisherman's wife. Chilling on the sand, watching the waves and the sunrise, resting, doing my own thing until I'm needed. Then, despite my best efforts and intentions, I'm not enough. I don't have what it takes to rescue those who need rescuing.

Most of all, I'm the seagull. Just trying to find something to satisfy my hunger, and I get hooked. I become fearful as I lose my bearings and my ability to fly. I'm dependent on others to help me get free. In my attempt to free myself, I become frantic. I fight and bite at anything or anyone trying to help me.

But there's another person in this story. The man who came in at the last minute and managed to unhook the seagull so it could fly again, unharmed. This man represents Jesus. He knows exactly what to do to free us. He will use any means possible to unhook us so we can continue to fly. Hallelujah, amen, and praise the Lord!

Be Complete

I hope you were able to see Jesus Christ in a deeper and more meaningful way by reading my stories. I am thankful for the moments I've had with Him.

Jesus is leading me moment by moment, feeding me day by day, and rescuing me more times than I would like to admit. I'm sure you've had moments like that with Him too. I suggest you write them down so you'll have something to look back on when you need a reminder of what He means to you and how only He can make you complete.

Chapter 8

TRUST THE HOLY SPIRIT

*H*ow do you know if you have the Holy Spirit guiding you? How do you know if you even have the Holy Spirit? Can you diminish the Holy Spirit in your life? Many Christians struggle with these questions.

The Holy Spirit has been with me since I believed in Christ. In my quest to get to know God for myself, I became more aware of the Holy Spirit's voice in my life. I have had instances where the Holy Spirit has directly spoken to me while writing and in dreams. I've also had moments when the Holy Spirit gave me very strong impressions about things.

When I started journaling, He answered many of my questions through various people. The Holy Spirit has led me to read certain passages and books that resonated with me strongly. The Holy Spirit also speaks to me through music and movies.

The Holy Spirit is like the wind. The Bible says the wind blows wherever it wishes, and so it is with the Holy Spirit (John 3:8).

Jesus states, "I will ask the Father, and He will give you another Advocate, who will never leave you. He is the Holy Spirit, who leads into all truth" (John 14:16–17).

In his book *Chazown*, author Craig Groeschel explains how to live life fully by finding, naming, and achieving your unique, God-given goal. *Chazown* is a Hebrew word for "vision," "dream," or "revelation." Groeschel provides a variety of ways to stay on course while pursuing God's *chazown*. One of those ways is fasting.

In the biblical book of Daniel, we find that he and his three friends went on a ten-day fast with only water and vegetables. Daniel was determined not to defile himself by eating the food and wine given to him by the king. Because he followed God, the Lord gave him and his three friends an unusual aptitude for understanding (see Daniel chapter 1).

As I was pursuing a vision for myself, I wanted to hear God more clearly on some things. I figured that a ten-day fast could help me with answers, wisdom, and understanding.

I was unsure what I was going to fast from. There are several foods I turn to for comfort or just because they taste good. I decided to stay away from bread, potatoes, peanut butter (one of my favorites), whipped cream (another favorite), and meat during my ten-day fast.

About a month before, I had started drinking hot herbal tea in the mornings. When I woke up on day 1 of my fast, I felt like I should not have that tea during my fast, so I refrained from it as well.

The first day went better than expected. I was able to go to bed without my bedtime snack.

The week I began my fast, I had begun a Fitbit step challenge. I started it on Monday, and Friday was the last day. I had 98,000 steps in so far and wanted to go for 120,000. But due to my fasting, I was exhausted.

As I prayed, I sensed that God wanted me to fast from exercise. "Seriously, Lord?" Exercise is a vital part of my life. I teach an aerobics class two days a week, and I get up early every morning to exercise. How could I fast from exercise? But that seemed to be what God wanted. So I laid that down too.

On day 2, my prayer journal entry reads:

Dear heavenly Father, I praise You for Your strength and guidance yesterday. I ask You to continue to guide and strengthen me as I walk with You. I pray that You will open my eyes and allow me to see wisdom and truth, especially with this book I'm writing. What stories have you placed within me to help others?

I'm feeling tired this morning, Lord. I cannot make it through this day without Your strength. Guide what I put in my body over the next nine days. Let it strengthen me and our relationship. In Jesus's name, amen!

Day 3

Dear heavenly Father, I give my dreams to you. What is Your dream for me? I want people to know of Your love and the satisfaction they can get when they follow You.

I want to know what my next step should be to accomplish Your purpose for me. Plant Your dream in me, lead me, teach me. What is our next move? *Our* meaning yours and mine. I don't want to move without Your guidance and companionship.

I feel like our next move is a restful, peaceful beach day together. Let's do that, Lord! In Jesus's name I pray, amen.

I took the *Chazown* book and my journal to the beach. This trip with God meant giving up spending the day with my family. But I needed the time alone with God. I needed to unwind.

Parts 1 and 2 of the *Chazown* book had me look at my core values, spiritual gifts, and past experiences to see how God has used all those things to push me to pursue His purposes for me. Now, in part 3, the author encouraged me to name my *chazown* and determine where to start.

I prayed this at the beach:

> *Dear heavenly Father, I'm here at the beach with You, looking for our dream. I believe You want me to dream big because You are big! Father, lead me and move me. When Jesus met the woman at the well, He knew all she had ever done and offered her living water. I am the woman at the beach. You know all I have ever done, and You offer me living water. Where have I dug holes looking for water and come up empty? How can my story help or lead others to Your love and forgiveness? What is Your purpose statement for me, Father?*

As I looked back through my journal reviewing my core values, spiritual gifts, and personal experiences, they all seemed to point to this purpose: to share God's love, His words of wisdom, and Jesus's truth of forgiveness, and to move others onto their path to Jesus so that their relationship with God can be restored and they too can return to innocence.

Now that I knew my purpose, I wondered how it was supposed to look. What was my first short-term goal? *What would You have me do, Lord?*

I wanted to have it named by the end of my fast.

On day 4, I had a relaxing day at home. I fasted from meat, starches, bread, peanut butter, hot drinks, and whipped cream. I ate lots of vegetables and fruits and drank plenty of water but no other liquids.

Day 5

Dear heavenly Father, I woke up this morning with fear and apprehension. What am I fearful of? I don't know.

Lord, guide my thoughts and actions today. Show me how to teach my standards at school with and through Your love. Nobody cares what I know until they know how much I care. Teach me how to do that.

What does Your list for me today entail? What would You have me do? I know. Pray. Do. Practice.

I had a hard day. I had some arguments with people I love. I was under spiritual attack. I needed all my emotional strength that day, and the Lord was with me.

Day 6

Dear heavenly Father, I sincerely love You and want to follow You. I desperately need Your Son to hold me and comfort me as I continue to fast and pray for the next few days. I need Your peace that passes all understanding in this matter.

I love You, Lord. I love the way You love me and protect me. I love the way You guide me by the hand. I praise You for Your voice and Spirit that lead me to rest in green meadows and lead me beside peaceful streams. You renew my strength and guide me along the right paths, bringing honor to Your name. Even when I walk through the darkest valley, I will not be afraid, for You are close beside me. Your rod and Your staff protect and comfort me.

On day 7, I woke up with severe gas pains in my abdomen. I didn't know what to do. I hurt so bad I couldn't even stand up straight. I prayed a lot, googled what to do with extreme gas pains, and did some stretching exercises. Eventually the pain subsided.

When I received a disturbing phone call, I knew I was under spiritual attack. It was coming at me from all sides.

After much crying, arguing, and praying, I went to work. A guest speaker was there waiting for me. I had scheduled her to come six weeks ago. I'd forgotten what she was there to speak about. Something to do with nutrition.

When she started talking about the dangers connected with certain foods, I knew God had placed her there for a reason. Her entire lesson was about the benefits of having a more plant-based diet.

What a perfect lesson for me to hear on day 7 of my fast, where I was eating a plant-based diet! It gave me confirmation that God was directing me through His Spirit.

Day 8

Dear heavenly Father, I praise You for revelation. I praise You for walking and running beside me, for guiding me, for giving me insights and might and the strength to persevere even in times of trouble and darkness. You alone are my hope and Savior.

During this ten-day fast, I was also on a ten-week weight-loss challenge at work. Each Thursday we were to weigh ourselves in front of someone. If we hadn't lost any weight that week, we had to give the person a dollar. The money went into a pot for the grand prize, which would go to the person who lost the most weight during the challenge.

On the morning of day 8, I felt a strong impression to not weigh myself. *Seriously, Lord?* But each time over the past eight days that I felt that still, small voice ask me to do something, I felt like God was asking me to choose between Him or myself. This day He was asking me to choose Him over my weight.

I didn't think I could do it, but I did. I walked up to my accountability person, gave her my dollar, and walked away without weighing in.

Day 9

Dear Father, I need a name for my online stuff and my overall ministry. A good, broad name that is specific to the overall purpose. My husband and I have been racking our brains trying to come up with a name for it, but nothing. Please put the name You want in my head. You know where You want this ministry to go and who you want it to reach. Put Your words in my mind and on my lips.

During this fast I was a culinary teacher, and we were learning how to make pizzas and bake sweets. How could I be on a fast from bread and sugar and do that?

To my complete amazement, the Lord gave me strength to say no to things on my list. There's no other way I could have accomplished it.

During these nine days, God had shown Himself to me in the small details just as He had done so many times before. He became more real to me, comforted me, and sustained me.

I prayed more than usual and asked Him to fill me whenever I would normally turn to food.

Day 10

Dear heavenly Father, I love You. Lord, thank You for guiding me through this fast. I praise You for filling me up with Your wisdom. I ask that You fill me with Your unfailing love and Holy Spirit. Guide my thoughts and actions today. Give me peace that passes all understanding. I feel empty physically. Take this pain of hunger from me, Father. Help me choose the right foods that will fill me up.

What would You have me write about, speak about, and call my website and ministry? Guide my thoughts and words. I keep praying this, Lord, because I want to get it right. Give me creativity and wisdom to show others Your love and show them how to move onto Your path.

I managed to eat only vegetables for breakfast and felt pretty good and full. Around four o'clock, when the time came to stop my fast, I felt led to keep it going until Sunday at church.

On Saturday, a dear lady gave me a red bag with tissue paper. I reached inside and pulled out a plaque with the words "grow old along with me the best is yet to be..."

On day 11, I got up, still unsure what I was supposed to name the ministry I wanted to begin. I had hoped to have it named by the end of my fast, but it hadn't happened. I questioned whether it would.

After getting ready for church, I climbed into my husband's truck and found a small envelope sitting on the floorboard. When I opened it, I realized it was a card that was supposed to go with the gift I received the day before. It must have fallen out when I pulled the tissue paper out of the bag.

I opened it and read the card. It had a small paper clipping inside. I read it to myself, "God is guiding you. Each of us has a divinity within us. When we see God working through us and with us, may we be encouraged, even grateful for that guidance. The Lord's hand is guiding you by divine design. He is in the small details of your life as well as the major milestones."

I read it again, this time out loud. When I did, my eyes focused on the words *divine design*. I said them a couple more times, then looked at my husband. "DivineDesign.me."

We both grinned, knowing that God had just named my ministry.

I grabbed my phone and did some research to find out where the excerpt came from. I read the entire sermon, and everything about it stood out to me as if I had written the message myself.

When we pulled up to the church, I saw the lady who gave me the card getting out of her vehicle. I told my husband to stop so I could get out and speak with her. I was so excited! I told her that she was a messenger of God in naming the ministry I wanted to begin. She said she gave that to me because there was a phrase that stood out to her that she felt in her spirit was meant for me. Praise the Lord, for He is good! His faithful love endures forever!

The fast is over, but something new has begun. I realize now that those feelings I get throughout the day, where I want more of something but cannot seem to figure out what, mean I'm wanting more of God, wisdom, Jesus, truth, the Holy Spirit, and understanding.

I'd been trying to fill that hunger with many things. When I finally turned to the Lord to fill my hunger, He gave me a taste of what only He can give. He helped me lay down things I was using to fill a hunger that only He can fill.

The next time you think you're hungry, send up a prayer and ask God to fill your longing the way only He can. You may need wisdom, a peaceful day at the beach, or revelation about something you've been wondering about. However He decides to fill you will be sweeter than honey.

You may be surprised at the places the Holy Spirit speaks to you. The Holy Spirit is wherever Jesus is. If Jesus goes to the temple, you will find the Holy Spirit there. If Jesus goes to a bar, you will find the Holy Spirit there. If Jesus goes across the ocean, you will find the Holy Spirit there.

When you first choose to believe in Jesus, you receive the Holy Spirit as a guide. As long as you continue to believe in Jesus, the Holy Spirit will keep leading you.

The Holy Spirit will not leave you if you go to the wrong place, think the wrong thoughts, or do the wrong thing. No, God's Word says we can grieve the Holy Spirit, but the Holy Spirit will not leave or abandon us. There are things that can get in the way of our hearing Him, but the Holy Spirit is always with us.

Have you experienced moments when you knew the Holy Spirit was guiding you? Write those things down so you can remember them and share them with others when the time is right. The Holy Spirit may use your story to encourage or love someone else.

Chapter 9

BE ACCEPTED, JUST AS YOU ARE

I can't believe what the scale told me last night. I haven't seen him in a while, and when I did, he told me I was fat and ugly. That was mean.

Has your scale done that to you too?

Usually, we try to stay away from the scale. But you can't always win at hide-and-seek, especially when your jeans are too tight for you to get to base before he catches you.

I struggle with self-esteem and body image. But instead of letting the scale influence how I feel about myself, I search for truth about who I am by listening to God. He tells me a different story.

After that scale was mean to me, my husband suggested we go outside for a walk. I went, but grudgingly.

As we walked, I realized that God has given me many strengths, but He gave me weaknesses too. Like my inability to be always 100 percent okay with my body image. But that's okay.

As I went to bed that night, I was afraid I would wake up the next morning and feel bad about myself for my weight. But when I got up and looked in the mirror, I thought, *I feel good. God loves me. Why am I always down on myself?*

I got out my prayer journal and wrote this:

Father, I praise You for reminding me who I am. I am Yours! I am wonderfully complex and perfectly imperfect, and that's the way You made me. You don't make junk! You even made the parts of me that I view as weak. I thank You for my weaknesses because they draw me to look to You. I find my perfectness in You. How

can I complain about something You created and said was good? I am Yours. I am a woman of God!

This truth is true for you too.

Psalm 139 is one of my favorite Scriptures. It reminds me of who I really am.

> *You made all the delicate, inner parts of my body and knit me together in my mother's womb. Thank you for making me wonderfully complex! Your workmanship is marvelous—how well I know it.*
> ~Psalm 139:13

> *How precious are your thoughts about me, O God.*
> ~Psalm 139:17

I choose to find my identity in God. When I give Him my hand, He leads me in His divine design.

Jesus meets us right where we are, wherever that is. When He walked the earth, He found a prostitute, a paralyzed man, and a leper, and He healed them. Whether we have run from Him, stomped on Him, or turned our backs on Him, He will come get us.

I love the novel *Redeeming Love* by Francine Rivers. It's based on the biblical story of Hosea and Gomer, and the story beautifully reflects the truth that Jesus is always faithful to us no matter how many times we leave Him. If you feel like you've sinned too much to be accepted by Jesus, forgiven by Him, or chosen by Him, you should read that book.

When I was a high school teacher, I was also the sponsor of Fellowship of Christian Athletes. In one meeting, they showed a video about how Hosea's devotion to the prostitute God chose for him to marry represents God's love for His bride, the church. These words in that video especially resonated with me:

> *As Hosea searched for his wife, Jesus came searching for the salvation of humanity. And when God found you, you were not*

so neat and put together. You were in chains, and you were naked, and you were sinful. And our gracious God says, "How much?"

The cost of our salvation was the blood of God's Son.

If God would only accept us after we found perfection, He wouldn't have sent Jesus Christ to save us from our flaws. Our works will never get us there (Ephesians 2:8–10).

The Bible is full of stories of God using imperfect people to rescue His children, to go to battle for Him, to spread His gospel. He accepts you and can use you, just as you are!

I like to get up early in the morning, sit by the window where the sun comes up, and spend time with the one being in the entire world who loves me completely unconditionally. As I sit there with Him, I tell Him all my troubles and worries, knowing I am precious in His sight. Having a peaceful moment with the Creator of everything is a wonderful way to start the day.

I encourage you to close this book right now and spend some time with God. Talk to Him about everything that's on your mind, then stay still with Him and contemplate how amazing it is that He accepts you, just the way you are!

Chapter 10

REST AND REJUVENATE

I'm looking at my to-do list for today and trying to figure out how I'm going to get twenty-eight hours of work done in twenty-four hours. And my entire week looks like this. I've got to let something go. But what can I give up doing?

As jam-packed as my agenda is, I have come to realize the importance of taking off one day a week from what I consider work. If I'm going to school, I don't write any papers that day. If I have a job, I don't do any work that day.

I'm not talking about extremes here. I still do laundry, the dishes, and other necessary chores. But I take a break from doing things I find stressful.

A few years ago, I was holding down multiple jobs and responsibilities while working on my master's degree. I didn't see how I could possibly get everything done if I didn't work seven days a week. Just thinking about taking a day off stressed me out. So I skipped several of my rest days over the course of a couple of months.

One Saturday evening, I felt strongly that I should take the next day off from doing schoolwork and trust that God would take care of it.

I had just turned in a paper and received a B on it. I wanted to work harder on the next assignment. Taking a day off would mean I'd probably get another B. But I took the day off anyway. I spent time with my family and had a good day of rest. During my prayer time, I asked the Lord to give me back the time I lost. "God, you are the owner of time. If anyone can give me back time, it's you."

I managed to finish my paper on time. And my grade was 100!

Coincidence? I don't think so. I believe it was God's way of showing me that I can trust Him.

Since that time, I have always taken one day a week off from school and work. When God calls us to do something, He gives us what we need to accomplish it.

In addition to working on my master's degree, I was a PIE (Program for Instructional Excellence) associate at Florida State University, a teaching assistant, and a full-time schoolteacher. I could not continue at that pace.

One day, as I was reading Scripture, I felt the Spirit tell me to give up the PIE associate position and the TA position. I didn't want to lose my waiver and have to pay for my last semester's tuition. But I had to trust that God would take care of my financial needs.

I left those positions. In January, I paid my tuition, hanging on to God's promise. In February I received a tuition waiver, and the college reimbursed me.

That year, I finished my master's degree (for free!), defended a thesis, passed with distinction, won an award as the top master's student in my program, was published by the *Journal of Communication and Religion*, was accepted to present my thesis at the National Communication Association, and received the top outstanding student paper award at NCA. I give God all the credit and glory!

I'm always amazed at what happens when I trust God. I'm also amazed at how long it takes me to take Him at his word.

> *God's promise of entering his rest still stands, so we ought to tremble with fear that some of you might fail to experience it. For this good news—that God has prepared this rest— has been announced to us just as it was to them. But it did them no good because they didn't share the faith of those who listened to God. For only we who believe can enter his rest.*
> ~Hebrews 4:1–3

The Holy Spirit gives us the ability to enter God's rest.

I normally like to rest on Sunday mornings. But one Sunday, I decided to go for a jog with my husband. I was tired and my body felt lethargic. I didn't even bother trying to keep up with him. I kept my own slow pace and just prayed and talked to God about things that were bothering me.

As I did, the word *rest* kept popping into my head. I felt like God was impressing upon me that His rest is better than my rest.

I pondered what I do to rest. Usually, it's watch TV or take a nap. Surely God's concept of rest must be much bigger than mine.

On the seventh day of creation, after He made everything, God chose to rest. He said, "Everything's looking good. I think I'll rest now." I realized that if God can rest, it's okay for me to do the same.

Something else came to my mind as I continued this *restful* jog.

I like food, and I often struggle with overindulging. But Jesus's living water is one thing we can't overindulge in. We never need to feel guilty about wanting more. We can soak in all we want!

When I got home from my jog, I read some Scriptures about God's rest.

> *At that time Jesus prayed this prayer: "O Father, Lord of heaven and earth, thank you for hiding these things from those who think they are wise and clever, and for revealing them to the childlike. Yes, Father, it pleased you to do it this way!*
>
> *"My Father has entrusted everything to me. No one truly knows the Son except the Father, and no one truly knows the Father except the Son and those to whom the Son chooses to reveal him."*
>
> *Then Jesus said, "Come to me all of you who are weary and carry heavy burdens, and I will give you rest."*
> ~Matthew 11:25–28

I love that God's Word says we are His children. I do feel like a child in many ways.

Because of the circumstances going on in the world, our burdens are many. We need this reassurance from Matthew that we can rest in Jesus and His love.

Jesus said:

"Take my yoke upon you. Let me teach you, because I am humble and gentle at heart, and you will find rest for your souls. For my yoke is easy to bear, and the burden I give you is light."

~Matthew 11:29–30

Let Jesus teach you. He will give you rest.

The next chapter in Matthew is a discussion about the Sabbath. Some people think we shouldn't do anything on the Sabbath. But Jesus looked at it differently.

Jesus was walking through some grainfields on the Sabbath. His disciples were hungry, so they began breaking off some heads of grain and eating them. But some Pharisees saw them do it and protested, "Look, your disciples are breaking the law by harvesting grain on the Sabbath."

Jesus said to them, "Haven't you read in the Scriptures what David did when he and his companions were hungry? He went into the house of God, and he and his companions broke the law by eating the sacred loaves of bread that only the priests are allowed to eat. And haven't you read in the law of Moses that the priests on duty in the Temple work on the Sabbath? I tell you, there is one here who is even greater than the Temple! But you would not have condemned my innocent disciples if you knew the meaning of this Scripture: 'I want you to show mercy, not offer sacrifices.' For the Son of man is Lord, even over the Sabbath!"

~Matthew 12:1–3

Jesus said when we're hungry, we get something to eat. Jesus Himself is that food for us.

When we need to rejuvenate, we can rest and feed on His love, which is far better than anything we could conjure up on our own.

Chapter 11

Expose Lies and Seek the Truth

I was contemplating what to read in the Bible today. I finished praying and asked God what He would have me read. I didn't hear anything from Him, so I opened my Bible and it fell to James. I started reading and immediately felt condemned. I continued reading and it didn't get better, so I shut my Bible and walked away discouraged. I thought, *Do I really want to follow the God who wrote this book?*

Has anyone taught you how to read the Bible? Have you experienced this scenario in your own life? Did you know there is a right and wrong way to read scripture?

It has taken me years to understand how God uses the Bible and how I should view it.

I didn't come to this realization on my own. *TheBibleProject. com*, Steve McVey, and other teachers and pastors opened my eyes to the truth about the Bible.

In our journey to expose lies and seek the truth, we need to understand how to read the Bible, remember we are under a new covenant because of Christ, test everything that is said, and think critically.

Understand How to Read The Bible

Growing up I had fun going to church. My Sunday school teacher always made the lessons engaging. The teacher used a felt board to tell some of the stories in the Bible. I was intrigued by stories of fish, whales, stones, and colorful jackets. One story even involved lions!

As I grew older and moved up to 3rd and 4th grade Sunday school classes, I learned quickly that if I could answer the questions about the Bible reading for the week then I would receive accolades from the teacher. Especially if I had the Bible verse of the week memorized.

Have you ever heard the phrase, "You don't know what you don't know until you know?" That is what happened to me over the years when it comes to understanding the Bible.

As I read in the Bible, I didn't understand it as a whole story. I didn't know that I could take a verse and use it out of context.

For example, when I read, "I can do all things through Christ who gives me strength (Phil. 4:13), I would believe that I could get stronger physically and mentally because Christ lives within me. That is not what that verse is referring to when we look at the verses surrounding it, who the author is, and who the author is speaking to.

The author is the apostle Paul, he is speaking to Christians in the town of Philippi, and he is speaking of being content. That he can be content in his circumstances because of Christ that lives within him.

We can see how easily we can take this scripture out of context though when we are doing something that requires mental or physical strength.

A couple of books that radically changed the way I read the Bible are *He Loves Me!: Learning to Live in the Father's Affection* by Wayne Jacobsen and *52 Lies Heard in Church Every Sunday* by S. McVey. These books helped me see God and the Bible in a different light.

In Jacobsen's book, I was introduced to the idea that God does not base His love for us on our performance for Him. Once I realized this, I started to read the Bible from a different lens. Instead of trying to find out what God wanted me to do for Him, I started looking for what God did for me. I started recognizing the acts of God throughout scripture. How God has loved me through the sending of His Son.

McVey, in his book, also kept me on the path of discovering

grace without performance, how to read the Bible, and finding worthiness apart from works.

I even found a website called the *Bible Project* that has been a useful tool for me in my quest to understand how to read the Bible and not take it out of context.

The Bible is one book that has many books within it. However, it tells one story: the story of Jesus Christ.

Reading the Bible will illuminate your sin and reveal that every person has sinned and fallen short of the glory of God. It is the universal human condition. Because of this condition, the Bible points you to Jesus Christ. He is the perfector of our lives. With Jesus Christ, you no longer live under sin or under the wages of sin, which is spiritual death. The sole purpose of the Bible is to point you to Jesus Christ. If it doesn't do that every time you read it, then you may be reading it with the wrong lens.

This morning I felt led to read in James. I have a study Bible that gives me verses in reference to the verse I am reading. I did some digging this morning in James chapter 3 and saw I am to examine what I say and what I do. If I look at this scripture through the lens that I must do these things to be righteous, I will see that I am failing. However, if I look at this scripture through the lens that I am saved because of Christ, and Christ is giving me desires to do the things that please Him, then I do not walk away feeling condemned. I walk away feeling empowered by Christ to do the things He has called me to do—like tame my tongue when I see my husband getting mayonnaise out of the jar, putting it on uncooked chicken, and then putting the spoon back in the jar.

I cannot do this on my own, and I cannot depend on myself to get it right. But I can depend on Christ who lives within me to help me tame my tongue when it's appropriate and be kind to my husband when I need to speak up.

When you open the Bible with the right lens, you can see it is full of problems. Most of those problems relate to human behavior, but some deal with disease and sickness that we have no control over. In the Old Testament we can see God attempts to deal with these problems through punishment. However, the punishment did not rehabilitate anyone. We also see that moral behavior and rules put in place for people to follow did not work or solve any of the problems either. So, what is the solution to all these problems scripture points us to? Jesus Christ. He is the only solution to all the problems in the Bible and in the world today.

Did you know when God looks at you, He sees Christ? He doesn't see just you! If he did, you'd be in trouble, and I would too. But that is not what He sees. He sees his perfect Son if you believe in His perfect Son. I love this about God and Jesus Christ!

Now Under the New Covenant

When we accept Jesus as our savior, we join the new covenant. There are several differences between the old and new covenants, and there are benefits to being under the new covenant. Under the old covenant we sacrificed animals to the Lord to be forgiven for our sins. We also found laws written on stone tablets and felt condemned when we didn't obey those laws. We were punished and had to work for our worth under the old covenant.

But now, we are under the new covenant. We have Christ as our sacrifice, and the laws are written on our hearts. We are accepted by God because of Christ, and we can rest in His love and sacrifice for us. We no longer must work for our worth but can allow our worth in Christ to work for us.

Under the new covenant we place our hope and faith in Jesus Christ. We no longer depend on our feeble attempts to obey, perform, and do works to earn salvation.

Without Jesus Christ there is no sacrifice for our sins. We must trust in Him for our justification before God and our salvation.

I created the following chart because I often forget we now live under the new covenant. When I get a flat tire or my prayers do not get answered, I begin to wonder what I did wrong and why God is punishing me. I must remind myself God is not punishing me or withholding anything good from me during those moments.

We no longer must sacrifice animals on a continual basis when we have sinned and want to ask for forgiveness—we have the blood of Jesus that paid the price once and for all instead. We no longer have laws written on stone that we follow, God's laws are written on our hearts. Under the old covenant we stayed condemned by God, but under the new covenant we are reconciled to God through Jesus Christ.

Old	New
Blood of animals	Blood of Jesus
Laws written on stone	Laws written on hearts
Work for fruits	Fruits flow from Christ
Continual sacrifices	One sacrifice (Jesus Christ)
Condemnation	Reconciliation
Letter of the law	Spirit of the law
If you do this then….	It is finished
If you obey then your accepted	You are accepted because of Christ
Punishment	Discipline
Performance	Rest
Working for your worth	You are worthy

Test Everything that is Said

One of the most terrifying stories in the Bible can be found in Matthew chapter 4. The Spirit led Jesus into the wilderness to be tempted by the devil, and the devil used Scripture and half-truths to tempt Him.

The Spirit will lead us into the wilderness, and the devil will use half-truths and Scripture to tempt us.

In the world today you will find many religions. A lot of those religions are based on Scripture and half-truths. How can you decipher who is right and who is wrong? How can you know beyond a shadow of a doubt you are on the right path in life?

There was a time in my life that I went into a different religion. As I went down that pathway, I could see a lot of truth in it. However, I also felt some error in what was being taught that did not resonate with my spirit.

I was very confused.

One day I was walking my dog, Muffin. I had her on a leash. We have a long driveway that turns into a limestone road that eventually leads to a major highway. When we got to the end of the driveway, I asked her which way she wanted to go. She tugged me to the left, but I wanted her to go to the right, so I started walking towards the right. She followed me. As we were walking away from the house, she would turn around to make sure I was there. The leash was not tight, and she could not feel my tug. Every few steps she would stop to make sure I was still with her. The closer we got to the major, busy highway, the more she would stop and make sure I was still there.

Once we got close enough to the highway, I tugged her to turn around. We made the turn, and she took off. The leash then became tight because she was walking so fast. As soon as she knew she was headed home she was in a hurry to get there.

God used this story in my life. This is how I felt when I went down that other religious path. I kept making sure God was with me. I kept looking at Him to make sure He was still with me. He was. Eventually as I got closer and closer to the highway, He tugged me to turn back and go home. I realized my only home is Jesus Christ. I feel the safest when I depend on Him for my salvation and my justification. This other religion added more to the cross than what I believed and what the Bible said.

I had to test everything said, and that brought me back to Jesus Christ as my only savior.

Think Critically

Jesus Christ is your personal savior. He is personal to you. He is your savior. He is your guide. He is guiding you by divine design. Based on the new covenant, the laws are now written on your heart and not on stone. Because of this, when making decisions you will need to listen closely to the Spirit within.

With billions of Christians in the world, we all have different views and experiences of what we would consider right or wrong. However, we can all agree on one thing: Jesus called us to love each other.

When faced with a decision, we can ask Jesus: is this the loving thing to do in this moment?

In today's world we have a lot of options when it comes to being fed spiritually. We can attend church virtually or in person or find devotionals in bookstores or online. We can even watch YouTube or other social media sites to feed our spirit. Because of the plethora of options at our fingertips, thinking critically is imperative.

Not Everything Sold as Truth Equals Truth

I had a time in my life when whatever was sold over the pulpit, I believed was intended for me to pursue. If the pastor said to sell everything and give it to the Lord, then I would do my best to sell everything. If the pastor said to be respectful to my husband, then I tried hard to respect my husband. Week after week there was something new I was needing to fix in my life. It became exhausting trying to live up to every sermon. I was so tired of trying to perfect myself that I walked away from the church.

Even though I walked away from church, I did not want to walk away from God. I started reading Christian personal development books everyday instead of going to church. I went from hearing a sermon once a week, to hearing a sermon daily.

This increase in sermons just perpetuated my dilemma.

God used this experience to show me not everything said in every sermon or book is meant for me to hear or apply to my life. I like to have everything planned out, but God said, "That's not how it works!"

This truth holds true for you, too.

You have to listen and discern the Spirit for yourself. You cannot hear and agree with everything because it may not be written on your heart.

This Scripture used to confuse me:

> *Think not that I am come to send peace on earth: I came not to send peace, but a sword. For I am come to set a man at variance against his father, and the daughter against her mother, and the daughter in law against her mother-in-law.*
> ~Matthew 10:34–35 KJV

I realize Jesus said this because if we all have the same rule book it is easy to get along, but if we all have a different set of rules God has placed on our hearts, then there will be some division within households.

We must filter our rules through Jesus's love. We may have differences of opinions when it comes to certain things, but we can all agree we should love others.

Jesus loved others through healing, forgiveness, touching those no one else would touch, talking to those no one else would talk to, and ultimately laying down his life at the cross.

We may not agree with things that our spouses, children, or friends believe is right or wrong or what they believe in, but we can still love them like Jesus loves by spending time with them, doing things for them, praying for them, and choosing to lay our selfish desires down to show them we love them.

Don't Give Up

If you find yourself having no desire to read scripture, it is very possible you are reading it with the wrong lens. I encourage you to not give up and find resources that can help you understand the context.

The process can be simple. Before I open my Bible, I pray to God. I ask the Holy Spirit to guide my thoughts and to guide me to the passage I should read for the day. Before I dive in, I will then watch a *BibleProject* video about that book of the Bible. It helps give me the context and overview of the book. Then I start reading with a prayerful heart. I do not take the words at face value. I dig, and I pray.

If I come away feeling the love of Jesus, then I know I've understood it. If I come away feeling condemned, then I know I've looked at it with the wrong lens.

Sometimes, I get confused and need to go to the internet to find clarification. There are several resources available. Don't give up because God has a message for you in his word.

Chapter 12

Feed Your Physical Health!

I hit the snooze button for the third time and roll over. I just do not have the energy or desire to get out of bed this morning. I pull the covers over my head, thoughts racing. *What do I have to do this morning? Can I sleep a little longer? I just do not want to face the day.*

I did not sleep well last night. I was up a few times tossing and turning. I had a bit of anxiety, and my heart was fluttering. I ate a bunch of sugary foods before bed. Why do I do this to myself?

I have found if I am pursuing my divine design then it must include my physical health. Our mind, body, and spirit are connected, but it is difficult to connect our flesh with our spirits when we are physically unhealthy. I know some things are out of our control. There are physical ailments that cannot be explained or helped. However, if we can make a difference in our physical health by what we put into our bodies and how much exercise we do, then it is important to try.

As I write this, I am in my fifties. I am at a time in my life where my hormones are changing, yet again. I also have been diagnosed with hypothyroidism. These conditions affect my metabolism which alters many things for me physically.

Throughout these changes in my physical health, I have learned some things I'd like to share with you.

Exercise Your Heart!

I have spent countless hours on body image and trying to obtain a certain look so people will accept me and love me more. However, I can tell you, it doesn't work in trying to achieve more value or worth from people or from God. God doesn't care what we look like, but He does care about our hearts.

We can find several Bible verses about the heart. Jesus says in John that rivers of living water can flow from our heart (7:38), He doesn't want our hearts to be troubled (14:1), and we can have a peaceful heart (14:27).

While God is more concerned about the emotional part of our heart, keeping our heart physically healthy is a wise idea too.

The World Health Organization recommends 150 minutes of cardio per week for adults aged 18–64.

I like to go for a walk and listen to music or the birds. I have found when I do this, I can hear God more clearly. What are some ways that you can have fun while getting your heart the exercise that it needs to stay healthy?

Get Strong!

Stop trying to lose weight and start trying to gain it by getting stronger. As we age, we start to lose muscle mass. To decrease the possibility of this, start lifting weights.

If you are new to weightlifting, then start gradually. You can begin by using water bottles or cans of green beans. Whatever you have on hand will do. You can begin with just your body weight by doing squats, push-ups, lunges, and sit-ups. You can do bicep curls with no weights to begin.

The purpose is to keep pushing yourself to the next level of strength.

For example, doing dumbbell curls with your own body. If you can do more than three sets of fifteen you will want to run to Walmart and grab some 2lb dumbbells or use water bottles. When you can lift those water bottles easily doing three sets of fifteen then you will want to move up to three or five lbs.

Keep a journal throughout this process. You will be astonished to see how strong you can get within six weeks. Whatever you do, do not give up! Consistency is the key when it comes to getting stronger.

You can join a gym if your finances and location permit you to do so. My husband and I have been going to Planet Fitness now for three or so years. We have both seen significant differences in our muscular strength and stamina.

You can also buy equipment to use at home if you'd like to save travel time and money in the long run. Amazon, Academy Sports, Dick's Sporting Goods, Walmart, Facebook Marketplace, and various other places can get you what you need.

Remember it is not about how you look, but how much stronger you will be getting.

Feed Your Muscles!

Instead of feeding your appetite, feed your muscles instead. Your muscles need food for fuel and growth which includes carbs, protein, and fat.

According to Examine.com, your protein, carb, and fat needs will vary based on your age, goals, and medical history. Examine. com is a database regarding nutrition and supplements that has over thirty researchers providing updated scientific findings. I suggest you check it out for more information on finding your own unique protein, carb, and fat goals.

Once you determine how much protein, carbs, and fat your body needs to maintain or build muscle, you can meal prep for the week.

You can find meal prep containers at most stores these days. It takes approximately an hour and a half to meal prep breakfast and lunch for my husband and myself for the workweek. Once you get the hang of it, you can do it efficiently.

When we take the time to meal prep, it makes it quick and easy to grab in the mornings on the way out the door.

On the weekends plan a couple meals when you can eat what you want. It is easy to eat healthy during the week when you know you can have a special dinner or treat on the weekend.

Keep a Journal!

Nothing can motivate you more than seeing your own progress. I like to keep a journal of my progress in strength, my food journey, and in pictures.

Nowadays almost everyone has a cell phone with a note app. Once a month while at the gym I will journal the amount of weight I am lifting and how many reps and sets. It is encouraging to see the numbers go up.

Keeping a food journal is important to ensure you are getting the protein, carb, and fat goals you set for yourself. There are several free apps available if you want to keep everything stored on your phone, or you can also use a paper journal.

Taking pictures of yourself with the same lighting and clothes on each time will also help you see your progress. I recommend taking a photo at least once a year. Be sure to include the front, back, and side views of your body.

See a Doctor!

I recommend seeing a doctor as regular as you can afford. Because I have hypothyroidism, I see my doctor every six months. She will check my thyroid levels, cholesterol, and a host of other things I have no idea how to pronounce.

Your body will tell you when you need someone else's opinion. Right before I found out I had hypothyroidism; I was experiencing different health issues. I was feeling fatigued, putting on extra weight, and my hair seemed to be thinning more than usual. My doctor was able to run some tests to find out what was going on. Menopause and hypothyroidism were the culprits and still are. However, the medicine has helped me live with these conditions without losing my mind.

Consider Medication!

Once you see a doctor, you may be prescribed some medications, or some supplements may be suggested to you. This is when prayer, trial and error, and common sense will need to kick in. If they suggest a medication, try it for yourself, pray about it, do some research, and see how you feel. Just because the doctor recommends it, doesn't mean it will work or it will benefit you. This is why I suggest praying about it, trying it out, and going with how you feel.

Take Small Steps!

Feeding your physical health doesn't have to be a challenge. Small changes along the way can make a big impact if you are consistent.

When I first began my health journey, I made small incremental changes. The first thing I did was cut out sodas. It was difficult at first, but eventually the cravings stopped.

Here I am, twenty years later, getting stronger and having the time of my life living out my divine design.

What is the first step you'll take to feed your physical health?

Chapter 13

Relax in Your Worth

Beware lest anyone cheat you through philosophy and empty deceit, according to the tradition of men, according to the basic principles of the world, and not according to Christ.
~Colossians 2:8 NKJV

While headed to the beach one morning, I passed by an old, run-down store and noticed a disheveled woman.

As I drove down the road towards my destination, I could not shake the quiver in my stomach to go back, so I turned around, got out of the car, and approached her. She was thin and looked like she had been crying.

She asked if I had $2 so she could buy a drink. I had bottled water with me and asked if she wanted one of those. She took one and took the $2.00 then I asked her if I could pray with her, and she told me yes. I put my arm around her and prayed and offered to take her somewhere, but she refused.

Finally heading back towards the beach, the feeling in my stomach subsided.

At the time, I did not ask her if she believed in Jesus or if she takes the political stance that I do. I did not care about those things in that moment. I just wanted her to know that she is worthy of someone's time and attention.

In my quest to find my divine design I have wondered about my worthiness and value and have been working for my worth in this world for a long time basing it on my performance and belief in Jesus Christ. I've been approaching my worth all wrong.

All Men are Created Equal!

Recently I attended a Civics class through the Florida Department of Education. During the course there was a section going over The Declaration of Independence. While I have read it before, something stood out to me that hasn't before. The Declaration states, "…that all men are created equal, that they are endowed by their Creator with certain unalienable Rights, that among these are Life, Liberty, and the pursuit of Happiness."

God created us, and because of that we have worth and are all worthy of love.

We are the Apple of His Eye!

As I was pondering being worthy of love as soon as we are born, the core of who I am came to mind, which made me think of the core of an apple.

The core of an apple has many toxins within it. Not only does it have toxins, but if you were to eat these toxins individually, they could kill you.

However, an apple not only carries toxins, but it also carries quite a few healthy things, too.

We are remarkably similar to the core of an apple. We are a mix of good and bad. Toxins are the sins in our lives: things that we have difficulty staying away from that we know will harm us in the end.

God knew when he made us that He was giving us the freedom to choose good or bad for ourselves.

One of the most profound ways that God shows His love, and our worth, is through the sending of His Son.

Before He even made the world, God loved us and chose us in Christ to be holy and without fault in his eyes. Jesus is the Lamb of God, slain from the foundation of the world, and while we were yet sinners Christ died for us! We are the apple of his eye!

I've had Five Husbands!

One of my favorite stories in the Bible is in John chapter 4, the woman at the well. She is headed to draw water from a nearby well but, when she arrives Jesus is there. As she puts her bucket down, Jesus asks her for a drink.

She is shocked that He would even talk to her much less ask her for a drink. She is fully aware of who she is and where she is from so, she does not feel valued, worthy, or loved.

Jesus tells her that if she knew who He was she would ask Him for a drink.

She doubts him at first but becomes curious when Jesus makes an offer that sounds too good to be true. He offers her living water: water that will never run out.

She decides to ask him for it. Jesus then points her to her sin, specifically asking her about her husband.

She admits she doesn't have one and Jesus says she is right, she does not have one.

She responds with the truth and Jesus confirms to her that not only does she not have a husband now, but she has had five husbands!

When Jesus says this, she immediately realizes that this man is not what He seems. He must be a prophet for Him to be able say these things about her life.

As I was reading this story, I pondered what women want in a husband.

A husband is supposed to be someone who loves and provides for me, has strength, is honest, and trustworthy.

I don't know about you, but I have created some "husbands" over the years that have not possessed any of those traits.

Husband #1: Man

When I was around 15 years old, I started to really look at boys. I wanted so bad to be seen, known, and loved by one. When I got the attention of a boy, who I deemed to be cute, it made me feel special and beautiful. Everything felt great until I realized they wanted something from me in return.

What I didn't see then, but I clearly see now, is that I was using them to fuel my need to be loved and confirmed while they were using me to fuel their need to have sex and feel like they had what it takes to be men.

I spent many waking hours trying to get a man to love me, take care of me, and provide for me—even if that meant controlling them to do so. I strongly pursued men who were hard to get, specifically, men who were not interested in who I was internally but who I was outwardly and what I could offer them as a woman who didn't know who she really was.

If I had the security of being in a relationship with a man then I felt loved, pursued, and somewhat satisfied, so I was willing to do whatever it took to stay in a relationship with a man.

I was taught to not have sex before marriage; yet I did. I was taught to not smoke cigarettes; yet I did. I was taught to not drink alcohol, drink and drive, and lie. Yet, I did!

I was digging a well where no water could be found. I was extremely thirsty but not finding any water in the holes I was digging for myself.

I was not finding the husband I was looking for either.

I ended up getting married but continued looking for love in all the wrong places. I put every bit of my need to be loved, confirmed, and provided for into my husband.

I failed in that pursuit. I was controlling, selfish, lustful, and immature. I searched for love in all the wrong places.

I must say here that I do not blame my ex-husband or my ex-boyfriends for the way I felt about myself during those times. Looking back on my life, I see that I was using them to fulfill a void in my life that I thought only a man could fill. I didn't realize at the time that I was being selfish and that I was using a divine desire that God placed within me to pursue Him to pursue the wrong things.

Husband #2: The Church

I finally got married again after four years of being divorced. I thought I found the right guy, and everything was going to start to get better now. Not too long after the honeymoon stage was over, we began having some of the same problems that I had faced before in my last marriage. I realized very quickly that I didn't want to go down the same path in this marriage, so I began to look at the common denominator—which ended up being me!

I realized that if this marriage was going to be different, I would have to make a change within myself. I started looking inward, asking myself what my faults were and what I could do to myself to make things better this time. After you keep running around in the same hamster wheel, getting nowhere, you begin to realize you should get off that hamster wheel.

I grew up in church and began to rebel against it when I started searching for man to fill those empty places in my life. I thought I knew how to love myself better than the church did. The church just felt very unloving and full of rules that I had to follow; rules I was having trouble even understanding. So, when I realized that my life was getting nowhere without the church and God, I decided I should go back to church. To be honest, I was not ready to go back. I just knew my new husband wanted to start going, so I hesitantly agreed because I liked the pastor of the church he wanted to attend.

Apparently, that's not the reason to go to church. I'm not saying here that this church is not of God. I believe that it is, but that is not why I was going to it.

The church we decided to attend was growing by leaps and bounds. It was innovative, creative, new, different, and exciting. It was everything that my life was not, and I wanted to be a part of it. Everyone did! If the pastor suggested it, I wanted to do it. Everything made sense from the teaching to the music to the ministries. I was totally on board!

After every sermon, I was ready to go home and make big changes for Jesus—or was it for the pastor? I'm not sure to be honest.

We began wanting to be a part of the church itself and its ministries. We knew if we were called to do one of the ministries, then we were good leaders and had good leadership qualities. We really wanted to do this for the church. It meant, for me, that we were significant people of the church if we could lead in it.

Eventually, we were asked to lead some ministries. I was a bit overwhelmed by it, but then I took it as my own. Even if I didn't believe in the purpose of the ministry, I tried to own the purpose. I made the ministry my identity.

Being a part of this growing church and being a leader of one of its ministries gave me fulfillment. I knew I was doing something for God, and it brought me significance and security I hadn't felt before. I allowed it to define me.

It was all great until it was taken away from me by the pastor. I was furious. I was exhausted. I was empty.

I was digging holes where no water could be found.

I dug hard this time, and I thought I was digging my hole in the right spot. I just knew this would get me the satisfaction I was looking for, but it didn't.

Husband #3: Outward Appearance

Another husband I have used to love me is my outward appearance.

I thought if I exercise and eat healthy then I can keep a certain body image. As I continue to live in this perishable container, I realize it is going to be a never-ending quest to find beauty and worthiness in this world if I base it on my looks.

I am tired of the fight.

As I continue to get older, it becomes more difficult to keep the wrinkles and pounds away.

On my 53rd birthday, my youngest daughter bought me a wellness journal. I decided I would give it a try.

One of the sections in the journal requires me to write a letter to myself giving myself the love that I give others. It also includes a section where I can give myself gold stars for the week.

Each week when I come to these sections I write something down about the things I have acomplished over the past week. It usually includes something like going to the gym, eating healthy, and checking off my to-do list.

Today, when I came to the gold star section, this is what I wrote:

I deserve a gold star for meal prepping and going to Planet Fitness, working on the Christmas show, and just being me.

I don't know why I never thought to write that last statement down before today. I believe it is because I have allowed body image to be my god and husband for so long that I do not know how to love myself for just being me.

Reviewing the past week, I wrote this letter to myself.

"Dear Elizabeth,

I love you just the way you are. An organized, driven, determined, kind, loving, creative, detailed, and analytical thinker, fighter, producer, director, music lover, writer, teacher, and researcher.

I am proud of you for loving yourself as is and for finding your worth internally instead of outwardly.

I know it is tough, but you can do this. I know Christ is with you and always will be.

Love,

Elizabeth"

Now would be a good time to put this book down and do this for yourself. Who are you? Who did God make you to be? Give yourself a little love and some gold stars!

"Who I Am" by Blanca is a great song to listen to when you are done.

Husband #4: My Career, My Doing

If I cannot find my worth in man and in my body image, then maybe I can find it in my career. I have been an educator since 2006, but that is not where I started.

Because of some of my earlier choices in life, I was unable to figure out what career I was interested in coming out of high school. I had some ideas, but nothing really stuck. There was a lot going on in my life, and I had no time to really think about a career

I've been a convenience store clerk, a life insurance salesman, a correctional officer, and a legal secretary just to name a few.

When I was little, I just knew I would grow up and be a teacher, but it took me a few years to come back to it. While working as a legal secretary, I felt the call within my spirit to teach. Within two weeks from the call, I was in a classroom teaching.

I was and still am a people pleaser. If my boss asked me to do something, I'd try my best to do it.

I was asked one afternoon if I would be willing to be the cheer coach. I did not want to do it, but because I am such a people pleaser, I could not say no. I dove headfirst into it and made it my identity.

I was willing to do whatever was asked of me and then some. I neglected my children and my husband because of all the requirements of being a cheer coach.

I had not cheered a day of my life. I was dependent upon other people to learn the ropes. I wish I could tell you that I was in it for the students, but I would not be telling the truth.

I found ways to have fun with it and encourage the cheerleaders, but at the end of the day it was about looking good in front of other people and my boss.

Yet another husband I created out of my insecurities and need to find satisfaction in this life.

Husband #5: My Purpose

Man, outward appearance, the church, and my career. None of those things brought me the satisfaction I was looking for, so I decided that it must be my purpose in life that I am missing. Maybe finding my purpose will help me find my worth in this world.

I started searching and asking God. I spent hours trying to figure out what God wanted me to do for Him in this world. What was His purpose for me? Surely if God told me His purpose for me, then I could work for my worth while working for Him.

As I was searching, God said to me, "go and get the husband you are married to now."

He wiped the mud off my eyes and showed me that anything I am using besides Him to fill my water jar will give me an empty water jar because He is the only one that can fill it up. It is His presence that I need in my life. Christ is my true husband, and being created and known by Him is what gives me my worth in this world

Let Your Worth Work for You!

I have worked for my worth in this world through many ways. Trying to uphold beauty and a certain body image. Trying to perform well within my job. Trying to perform for God at church and through a ministry. Trying to find it in my purpose in life. But God says, you have had worth since the day you were born.

I am worthy because God formed me in my mother's womb. I am worthy because he gave me life and breath. I am worthy because even before He knew the choices I would make; He sent His son to die for my sins.

Today I rest in my salvation and in God's love as I live in this world. I do not have to work for my worth anymore. I can allow my worth to work for me.

I call this *active rest*.

Active rest means walking through life, doing the things you feel the Holy Spirit is leading you to do, and knowing full well that even if you don't do it, you are still worthy of love and acceptance because God loved you so much to send His Son into the world to save you.

Discussion Questions by Chapter

Chapter 1: Pray
- Talk about a time in your life when you didn't want to pray or didn't think to pray.
- Do you ever get distracted while praying? What could help you stay focused?
- Do you have a prayer warrior in your life? If no, who could be one for you?

Chapter 2: Control Your Mind
- Do you spend more time on death thoughts or life thoughts throughout your day? Explain.
- What are some scriptures that you use to pump you up spiritually?
- In what ways will you remind yourself of the truth of God's word daily?

Chapter 3: Know you have an enemy
- Where does the enemy tend to try to steal your joy in life?
- What does the enemy bring up from the past that still haunts you today?
- Talk about a time when you listened to the wrong voice. What was the result of that?

Chapter 4: Figure out what is weighing you down
- How do you push forward when things get tough?
- How do you manage your time?

- Have you ever disagreed with someone yet remained silent? Why or why not?

Chapter 5: Remember who you are
- What type of situation makes you forget who God says you are?
- How do you remember who God says that you are?
- What are some action steps that you can take to remember who God is?

Chapter 6: Know God Loves You
- How have you built your relationship with God over the years?
- What are your love languages? Do you see God loving you in those ways? Explain.
- Do you believe God loves all the parts of you? Why or why not?
- What songs remind you of God's love?

Chapter 7: Sit at Jesus Feet
- Tell a story about a time when you sat at Jesus feet.
- Tell about a time when Jesus freed you from bondage.
- Is there any area in your life that you have not forgiven yourself?

Chapter 8: Know the Holy Spirit is guiding you
- Talk about a time when you know the Holy Spirit was guiding you.
- How do you discern if it is the Holy Spirit's guide or your own?
- Talk about a time you fasted, what from, why?

Chapter 9: Be accepted just as you are
- Do you accept yourself just as you are? Why or why not?
- Do you find it hard to believe that Jesus died on the cross for all people-no matter their sin? Why or why not?

- Where to you tend to find your identity in this life? What have the results been?

Chapter 10: Rest and Rejuvenate
- What do you do to rest?
- Do you take a day off every week? Why or why not?

Chapter 11: Expose Lies and Seek the Truth
- Talk about a section of the bible that has or does confuse you.
- What lens do you approach the bible with on most days? (Love, judge, self-help book)
- Where do you go when confused by scripture for clarity?
- Which covenant does your mind having you living under? The old or new?

Chapter 12: Feed your Physical Health
- In what ways do you feed your physical health?
- How can you improve your physical health?
- In what ways do you measure your physical health?

Chapter 13: Relax in your worth
- In which area have you been digging holes where no water will bubble up? (career, man, purpose, church, marriage, being a parent, your ministry)
- What do you need to put down or stop doing because you are working for your worth in this world?

Acknowledgements

I didn't know what I was getting myself into by writing a book and the encouragement it would take to get me here. I couldn't have done it alone!

First, I give thanks to God. He is my energy, breath, love, companion, provider, healer, guide, wisdom, and creativity.

To my husband, Daniel, thank you for your unwavering love, patience, and support. Your belief in me has been a constant source of strength.

To my parents, Bob and Patty, for always loving me, even when I made it hard. Thank you for your unwavering childlike faith in Jesus and for instilling your faith into me.

To my daughters, Dianna and Breeanna, thank you for loving me, listening to my advice (whether you wanted it or not), and for the thought-provoking conversations we've had. Your presence in my life has saved and enriched my life in many ways. To Brett (Dianna) and Brenner (Breeanna), thank you for walking beside my girls and adding value to our family.

To my grandsons, Eric Michael and Ryder, may you always be reminded that your lives are part of a divine design, filled with purpose and worth and that I'll always be proud of who you are.

To my favorite authors, Wayne Jacobsen, Steve McVey, and John and Stasi Eldredge, thank you for helping me discover that I am fully loved by God, even if I never wrote a book, created content, or attended church.

To my editor, Kathy Ide, your detailed and time-consuming edits made this book a more compelling read. Thank you for being kind to me as a novice author. I also want to thank my daughter, Breeanna, for stepping in to edit and offering her thoughtful perspective along the way.

To my publisher, Mike Parker at WordCrafts Press, thank you for walking with me through the publishing process and for taking me on as a first-time author. Your work in preparing this manuscript for print has made the vision for this book a reality.

To my deeply conversational friends and cheerleaders, Tracy Ippolito, Dottie Strong, Rose Marie Cloud, Stephanie Van Clief, Laurie Stump, Angela Donahue, Cindy Lee and my hairdresser, Courtney Bass, your encouragement has meant the world to me and kept me moving forward-one conversation at a time. To Krista Beckwith, Linda McClellan, and Mary Solano for taking the time to read my first draft and give me some uplifting feedback.

To Marilyn Nutter, for reminding me that something worthwhile is worth the wait.

In memory of Faye Eubanks, who trusted God, leaned not on her own understanding, heard His still small voice, and followed through with handing me His message, which ultimately named this book.

Finally, to my readers, thank you for taking a chance and engaging with this book. It is my prayer that its message strengthens your faith, deepens your sense of identity, and equips you to live fully in the divine design God has just for you.

About the Author

*E*lizabeth May Bennett has been an educator for over twenty years in a variety of subjects and mediums including Christian studies, public speaking, media writing, leadership, critical thinking, reading, physical education, coaching, and aerobics. She resides in a small town in Florida and works from home as an online instructor.

Elizabeth received her master's degree in communication at Florida State University and was awarded the Outstanding Paper Award at the National Communication Association Convention in 2021. She has been published in the *Journal of Communication and Religion* for her thesis on understanding the role of prayer and relationship with God for Christians before and after the death of a child.

In her spare time, she creates content for her social media platforms and enjoys spending time with her husband, children, and grandchildren, reading, writing, and going to the beach.

Connect with Elizabeth online at:

www.elizabethmaybennett.com
facebook.com/divinedesign.me/
instagram.com/divinedesign.me/
tiktok.com/@divinedesign.me
youtube.com/@divinedesignme

Also Available From

WORDCRAFTS PRESS

Learning as I Go
by Christy Bass Adams

In the Boat with Jesus
by Marian Rizzo

God in the Commonplace
by Beverly Clopton

Illuminations
by Paula K. Parker

When the Other Boot Drops
by Jeff Keene II

The Gift of Peace
by Kira Marie McCullough & Keb Burns

www.wordcrafts.net